AF371874

GHOSTS OF THE UPPER FLOOR
THE COMPLETE *DARK SHADOWS*
(OF MY CHILDHOOD), BOOK 3

GHOSTS OF THE UPPER FLOOR
THE COMPLETE *DARK SHADOWS*
(OF MY CHILDHOOD), BOOK 3

TONY TRIGILIO

BLAZEVOX[BOOKS]
Buffalo, New York

Ghosts of the Upper Floor
The Complete *Dark Shadows* (of My Childhood), Book 3
by Tony Trigilio
Copyright © 2019

Published by BlazeVOX [books]

All rights reserved. No part of this book may be reproduced without the publisher's written permission, except for brief quotations in reviews.

Printed in the United States of America

Interior design and typesetting by Geoffrey Gatza
Cover design by Michael Trigilio

First Edition
ISBN: 978-1-60964-337-9
Library of Congress Control Number: 2019930782

BlazeVOX [books]
131 Euclid Ave
Kenmore, NY 14217
Editor@blazevox.org

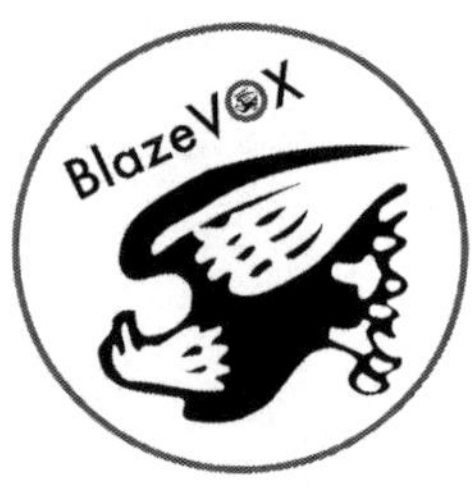

publisher of weird little books

BlazeVOX [books]

blazevox.org

21 20 19 18 17 16 15 14 13 12 01 02 03 04 05 06 07 08 09 10

BlazeVOX

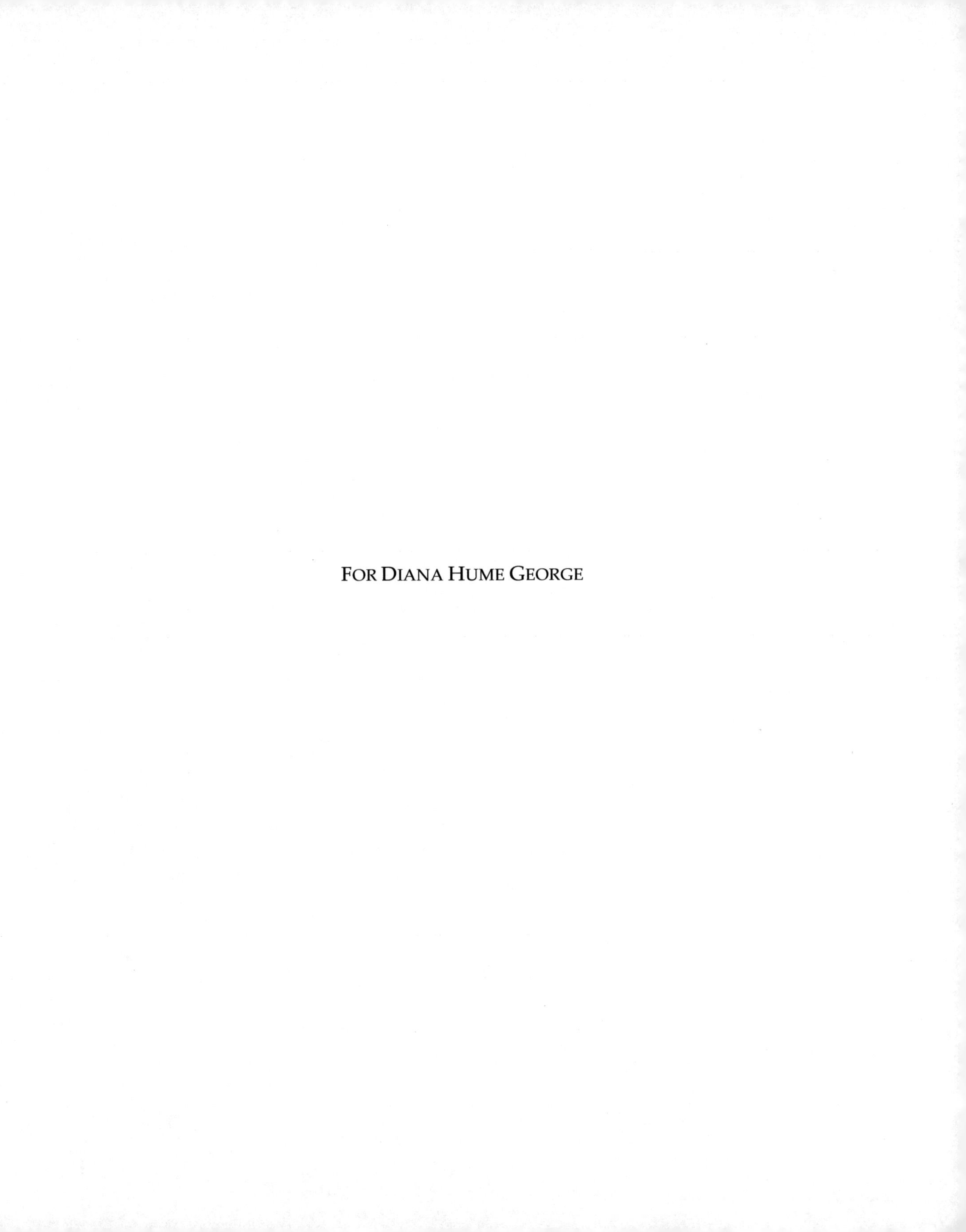

For Diana Hume George

Table of Contents

GHOSTS OF THE UPPER FLOOR:
THE COMPLETE *DARK SHADOWS*
(OF MY CHILDHOOD)

BOOK 3

Behind the Scenes: My Barnabas Collins

Dark Shadows was a soap opera broadcast weekdays on the ABC television network from 1966-1971. The show set itself apart from other daytime soaps with its relentlessly gothic aesthetic and plotlines built around ghosts and other supernatural phenomena. The uncanny became a permanent feature of *Dark Shadows*. It remains the only haunted soap opera in American TV history.

On April 17, 1967 (Episode 210), the show introduced the character of Barnabas Collins, a vampire from the eighteenth century accidentally freed from his chained coffin in 1967 by a grave robber, Willie Loomis. The show's producers originally intended to keep the Barnabas character around for only a 13-week narrative arc. But he quickly became the most popular character on the show, and he remained a central figure from April 1967 through the show's cancellation in 1971.

Barnabas Collins was the star of nearly all my childhood nightmares. I watched the show every day with my mother, a devoted soap opera fan, in the first months and years of my life—and many of my earliest memories are terrifying recollections of Barnabas stalking me. I was petrified by Barnabas; at the same time, the vampire also was an object of insatiable curiosity for me. My feelings about Barnabas were nurtured and sustained before I came into language, and are twined with some of my most primal sensations.

Production Notes

This is the third book of a multivolume experiment in autobiography. I intend to watch all 1,225 episodes of *Dark Shadows,* composing one sentence for each episode and shaping each sentence into verse or hybrid form. Book 1 began with Episode 210 (Barnabas rising from the dead) and ended with Episode 392. Book 2 features Episodes 393 through 573. Book 3 resumes with Episode 574 and continues through Episode 695. As in Books 1 and 2, the epigraphs at the beginning of each section of Book 3 are taken from the *Dark Shadows* introductory teasers spoken by individual characters in voice-over at the beginning of each episode.

I will return to Episodes 1-209 in the final volume, as a kind of prequel/coda, after I have watched the last episode of the series. The show was preempted 20 times during its five-year run, and in these instances the network double-numbered or triple-numbered the episodes so that the show airing on a Friday would always end in a 5 or a 0. The final episode of *Dark Shadows,* then, is officially Episode 1,245, even though it was actually the 1,225th episode produced for the show.

The author wishes to thank the editors of the following journals in which excerpts from this book appeared, often in different versions: *Columbia Poetry Review, Dispatches from the Poetry Wars,* and *Fifth Wednesday Journal.* Warm, undead gratitude to Jan Bottiglieri, Matthew DeMarco, Ellipsis Coffeehouse, Geoffrey Gatza, Chris Green, Liz Shulman, Michael Trigilio, and David Trinidad.

Previously in *The Complete* Dark Shadows *(of My Childhood)*

I'm still stuck in 1795.

Liz and I watch Barnabas die.

I mark the one-year anniversary of Barnabas's first appearance brooding over the
DVD extras.

"I'd like to see Barnabas turn into a vampire," Liz texts from New York.

I'm not as brainy-tough as I thought, if a stranger in a Spiritualist chapel in the plains
of rural Indiana can bring my dead mother back, talking more lucidly than she did
after her stroke.

A night of multiple rewinds to confirm I actually saw a stagehand tap a yellow
wrench against a machine buzzing in Dr. Lang's Frankenstein laboratory.

I'm a future dead person, but I want to finish the poem before I'm tucked into my
coffin.

Add corpse putrefaction to the list of horrors I learned as a child from *Dark Shadows*.

Mothers of America, let your kids go to the movies—get them out of the house so
they don't have to see a TV show that routinely buries its characters alive and now
just executed an innocent woman in slow, excruciating detail.

My god, it's still 1795.

"After reading your poem last night, I awoke this morning and found a fucking bat
sleeping on a window blind inside our living room."

One hundred sixty more episodes to go until the show's first werewolf.

Director Lela Swift, queen of the premature burial trope, sends away the Old House
set for minor repairs and someone from ABC mistakenly takes it to the dump to be
burned.

If only my childhood *Dark Shadows* nightmares could have been so obviously staged as the terrors of Cassandra's dream-curse.

I list all the obsessive-compulsive steps required before I can actually leave the apartment on any given day, and the total is 39.

Unlike in *Dark Shadows*, sometimes we actually experience the uncanny with dignity, as when my brother turned to his wife in their living room at the moment of his death and said, simply, "Thank you."

Step number 40 before I can leave: if I don't scratch our two cats atop their heads before I depart each day, one of them will die while I'm gone.

I feel disembodied, waiting out the storm in what I'll soon call my former office—last box packed, tornado bearing down, sky black and purple.

The possibility that pleasure might be enforced upon me, inflicted against my will as part of a performance as intricately stylized and symbolically charged—and erotic— as anything from our Sunday Mass rituals of discipline and punishment and blood and wine and mortification.

Rhyming couplets, a birthday gift for myself.

"I don't like that part about me: I'm only in the poem because I asked to be," Liz says, adding, as I transcribe her words, "and now you're going to keep quoting me."

All the cities in which I saw the poem's first 357 episodes: Chicago (299); Evanston, Illinois (18); San Francisco (7); Paris (5); Durham, New Hampshire (4); Milwaukee (3); Middelburg, the Netherlands (3); Seattle (3); Madison, Wisconsin (2); Los Angeles (2); Pittsburgh (2); Iowa City, Iowa (2); Lawrence, Kansas (2); San Diego (1); Chesterfield, Indiana (1); Boulder, Colorado (1); Boston (1); Fort Wayne, Indiana (1).

Barnabas's purple smoking jacket swarming with fuzzy, ovoid shapes that resemble raindrops or amoebas or purple ladybugs.

A *Dark Shadows* spirit guide looking out for us, manipulating this mortal world for maximum kitsch.

I'm Jack Spicer listening for radio signals from beyond, prepared to take dictation from his Martian muses, watching for a *Dark Shadows* epiphany.

Endless, plodding story lines that do nothing but enact, over and over, how ill-equipped we are to navigate the rudimentary intimacies of human relationships.

Only 90 episodes until the first werewolf appears.

GHOSTS OF THE UPPER FLOOR
THE COMPLETE *DARK SHADOWS*
(OF MY CHILDHOOD), BOOK 3

Nothing was more natural than that these things should be the other things they absolutely were not.

—Henry James, *The Turn of the Screw*

1.

Night over Collinwood. A dismal night that promises new disasters.

Halloween, 2015, Book 3 begins inside a claustrophobic box of prose—anxious that I've abandoned the couplet—watching *Dark Shadows* with Liz and David Trinidad, my neighborhood, Rogers Park, overrun by vampires, witches, zombies, demons, and drunk Loyola students: Joe demands that Maggie turn down the shades (twice bitten by Angelique, he shrinks from the rising sun), and soon, I imagine, all of Collinsport's curtains will be drawn, the town crawling with vampires, and no one will walk in daylight; "This is 'The Brown Episode,' Tony," David says, pointing out Maggie's brown barrette, Joe slumped in front of his varnished brown door, his chin pressed against the brown bedpost as he stares at Maggie's brown-and-white checkered empire dress—her brown handbag lying on the bed—Angelique's vampire poison surging through his veins; next scene opens with Willie Loomis knocking at Maggie's door, nervous and lovestruck, his scruffy, brown suede jacket wrinkled by tics and jitters.

An oscilloscope flanked by a pulsing round orange light, empty beakers, an operating room spotlight, a preposterous neon laboratory prop (two tuning forks welded together and blinking short, random bursts of fluorescent pastel, their chalky pink luminosity more suitable to *Miami Vice* than the gloomy lair of daytime soap opera mad scientists): surrounded by an electronic junk pile designed to bring Adam's Bride of Frankenstein to life, Jeff Clark pores over Dr. Hoffman's laboratory notes and swipes at a soundstage fly buzzing his left ear.

On my way to Norway, invited by art
historian Frida Forsgren to deliver

a lecture on Elise Cowen at the University
of Agder, my connecting flight from

Copenhagen leans into the Danish
overcast, ascending, the misty grass

recedes as we disappear into cloud
and a fat shaft of morning sunlight

(after an eight-hour overnight flight
from Chicago), turboprop rumbling

out the window, our cramped cabin
vibrating as I read, the most recent jolt—

stomach-dropping turbulence, churning
through a dim, gray mass of clouds—

jerks my hand across the page, slashing out
an entire paragraph while trying to underline

my favorite passage in James Shea's review,
in the latest *Pleiades,* of W.S. Merwin and

Takako Lento's Buson translations:
haiku poets immerse themselves in

what James calls "the dignity of the particular,
both rendering the particular and evoking

something greater than it"—then another
particularly light-headed dip into the jet-

stream tumble, and as I clutch the armrest, take
deep breaths to prevent myself from visualizing

an outright plummet, it occurs to me
James is describing what my impossible

object of a poem (which has now returned,
briefly, to the belovèd couplet as an homage

to his essay and a reminder I'm not ready
to abandon the form just yet) aspires to,

even though, later tonight in my room
at the Hotel Norge, *Dark Shadows* will

"render the particular" with anything but
dignity: "Labour well the Minute Particulars,

attend to the Little-ones," Blake wrote
in 1820 in *Jerusalem*, a vision of science

and art that will unfold 148 years
later in flashes of meaningless blue

waves on Jeff Clark's oscilloscope
and an inexplicably tight close-up

of Roger's sherry glass—alcoholic fetish
object we won't really see, the camera

immediately heaving into a backward
tracking shot that reveals Roger standing

over Vicki, who, seated politely on the sofa,
cannot refuse another refill, Roger offering

a lushy toast to celebrate Vicki's engagement
to Jeff (who, as they clink glasses, swoons,

trapped in Hoffman's laboratory with
Angelique, who sinks her fangs into

his neck) while the camera wobbles,
still not recovered from the rough patch

of turbulence that caused its backward
lurch away from Roger's sherry glass;

watching in my dark hotel room, jet-lagged,
15 hours after taking off from Chicago,

the sound of giant boots clomping offstage
drowns out Roger's speech to Vicki as he lifts

a second glass of sherry to his mouth
(awkward cut to three-second close-up

of Jeff's twined pink neon tuning forks),
and later, Mrs. Stoddard labors well

the minute particulars of her burial dress,
still consumed by fear she'll be buried

alive (yes, the queen of the premature burial
trope, Lela Swift, directed this episode)—

and the camera spontaneously rolls leftward
(all of a sudden, I need Dramamine to watch

Dark Shadows), fleeing the only actor
in the shot as she considers a moss-green

and purple paisley dress; eventually,
she chooses a dour black one, of course,

perfect for the next scene's terrifying
dream sequence: the camera stationed

above an open casket containing her
body, Roger and Carolyn grieving,

and Mrs. Stoddard paralyzed, unable
to let them know she's actually alive

before Roger can close the casket
(no wonder that when I witnessed

my grandmother's head bolster lowered
and her coffin lid closed, age 15, I feared

the funeral director was burying her
alive, and I, as a pallbearer, bore partial

responsibility—weeks of sleep paralysis
and nightmares followed); "Why can't I

speak," Joan Bennett's (Mrs. Stoddard's)
voice-over whines, "why can't I move—

they're going to bury me alive," but Joan,
unable to hold still and stay in character

and play dead for just a few more seconds
of tonight's final scene, until the credits roll,

blinks and twitches her mouth.

Stark choices for pre-cable era daytime television viewers on 9/10/68, the 4:00-4:30 time slot occupied by slapstick escapism on CBS (*Art Linkletter's House Party*), inane game-show banter on NBC (*The Match Game*), and a contemporary primal-terror remake of Poe's "The Premature Burial" on ABC: Mrs. Stoddard repeats her nightmare from the end of the previous episode, but for some reason she wakes this time beneath the black-and-green afghan last seen draping Maggie Evans's sofa at the end of Book 2 of this poem (four episodes ago), which, as I explain to bandmates Brian Cremins and Allison Felus, watching tonight with Liz and me after a vegan Thanksgiving feast—chana masala, palak paneer (tofu deliciously masquerading as cheese), two salads (kale massaged with avocado, and romaine drizzled with tahini-mustard-lemon dressing), mocha pecan pie, and peanut butter cookies—is the same afghan that, back in 1795, covered Jeremiah and Josette's bewitched marriage bed at the Collinsport Inn; "My coffin is to be in the center of the room, resting on a marble base," Mrs. Stoddard says later to Lawyer Peterson, dictating an amendment to her will inspired by the narrator of Poe's premature interment yarn (if only, age two, I had an attorney who, like Peterson, could've written a legal document establishing a series of funereal safeguards that would prevent anyone in my family from accidentally burying me alive), "by no means must there be any marble around the coffin ["What does *that* mean?" Liz asks when the two of us rewatch this scene the following day, adding, "It's like she doesn't want any other marble to take away from the beauty of *her* casket"]: the coffin is to be specially made—there are to be small air vents where my head will abide, and inside the coffin, there will be a buzzer, which, when I press it, will release the lid of the coffin and simultaneously start a bell ringing; the bell will be in the tower and must be loud enough to be heard everywhere in this house" ("I can't believe you live in this world—with these people

you just go and visit all the time," Allison says
afterward, an ars poetica for my 848 episodes
remaining).

Carolyn, whose mother is scared to return to Windcliff Sanitarium because she's sure the psychiatrists want to bury her alive, was interrupted yesterday at Collinwood's tinkling pee-pee fountain by her ex-lover—her mother's attorney—while reading Freud ("To many people the idea of being buried alive while appearing to be dead is the most uncanny thing of all," he writes in his famous essay "The Uncanny," where he also describes "the double," or the divided self, as a "ghastly harbinger of death"), and today she's played by an entirely different actress, Diana Walker, taking over Nancy Barrett's role for one episode—her first and only *Dark Shadows* appearance.

Variation on the soap trope Liz first explained to me four years ago, when we watched Episode 288: Barnabas stares at the back of Professor Stokes's right shoulder as Stokes talks to the back of Jeff Clark's neck while Jeff gazes into a seven-branched candelabra; later, Vicki talks to Jeff's back, concentrating on his shoulder blades like they're a microphone, but looks him in the eye when she returns his engagement ring.

"I don't want to mate anymore," Adam says to Nicholas Blair as a bobbing, motion-sick camera follows him into the parlor of the House by the Sea.

Watching *Dark Shadows* with Liz on our hotel bed in San Diego, laptop perched on my thighs—a day of freezing temperatures, torrential rain in Southern California (climate-change weather mutations, 55 tornadoes and massive flooding this week in the South and Midwest, one tornado so strong it ripped the carpet off the floor of a Memphis home)—and Adam, the artificial man, tiptoes into Carolyn's bedroom in brown Hush Puppies but wakes her anyway, his corpse-stitched face later falling into a boyish, Sal Mineo pout when she rejects, yet again, his clumsy sweet talk; we finally get to see Hoffman's *Bride of Frankenstein* lab in action, a cockamamie Rube Goldberg device of coils, oscilloscopes, two pink tuning forks yoked together, a glass tube— trembling as it fills up with mysterious brown liquid—non sequitur light bulb close- ups, and the vampire Angelique strapped to the operating table. Angelique, jolted by body-shaking electromagnetic bursts ("This would really give you nightmares," Liz says, "it's like the electric chair") beneath overexposed, red-and-pink-tinted stage lighting, accompanied by radio static, arrhythmic electronic pings, and a repeating squishy sound like a finger scratching a tinfoil ball swept through a flanger—a discordant symphony interrupted by Barnabas, standing before the same brick wall where, in 1795, he immured Reverend Trask in one of the show's earliest premature burials.

More goth-soap somatic commotion, Willie takes writer
Sam Hall's alliteration a little too seriously: "These
people, they got *plans* for you!" he says to Maggie, her
hair puffing backward from the force of his consonants.

"A woman brought me into the graveyard to find out if I remembered being here before," Maggie says to Willie, after waking, confused, in the secret room of the Collins family tomb; "it's like a maze, trying to remember a place, trying to remember"—then a cheaply cobbled audio jump cut intrudes and Maggie's prerecorded, lo-fi voice-over narrates her flashback to the night, 301 episodes ago, when Dr. Hoffman escorted her to Eagle Hill Cemetery, shock treatment for the amnesia Maggie suffered after escaping the vampire who'd kidnapped her (a dose of goth science, prescribing a midnight graveyard stroll to cure post-traumatic memory loss): "It was dark," Maggie continues, "it rained that day—the smell of it was still in the air, carried by a cold, biting wind"; Maggie's aromatic memory of petrichor, the plant-oil and geosmin mixture released from soil when it rains, becomes my madeleine ("No sooner had the warm liquid mixed with the crumbs touched my palate," Proust writes of the tea/pastry mixture that triggers his exquisite unfolding of memories, "than a shudder ran through me and I stopped, intent upon the extraordinary thing that was happening to me"), transporting me instantaneously to the location, my family's TV Room, where I originally watched this episode with my mother on 9/19/68 (yes, Maggie, "it's like a maze, trying to remember a place, trying to remember"), back when owning a television was such a novelty

                    we named an entire room in our home
after this central technological object which we'd arranged the sofa and other furniture around: a 12-inch black-and-white (even when the show was broadcast in color, we watched monochromatically, each episode resembling the washed-out kinescope videotape copies I've written about in Books 1 and 2, and we couldn't afford a color TV until I was in first grade, after *Dark Shadows* had been cancelled) shoved against the west wall picture window that looked onto our tiny backyard and the sycamore whose hornet's nest petrified me every summer; our oafish chest freezer loomed between the television and back door, its lid secured with a stubborn gasket seal that made it impossible for a small child to lift, no matter how many times I imitated Willie Loomis straining to open Barnabas's casket, the airtight, freezer-sealed coffin lid preventing my pilfering of the Neapolitan ice cream my mother never failed to stock along with

popsicles and freezer pops inside the chest freezer in the room where she had her stroke 31 years later, when the gray-and-white, sausage-rope carpet weave became predatory, her brain splitting into blood hemispheres beneath the diamond-shaped ceiling lights my parents special-ordered in 1965, which I mistakenly recalled as 1962 in "Thinking While Held Down," from my first book of poems, *The Lama's English Lessons*—

       "I remember one gravestone in particular," Maggie continues, "I remember being terribly frightened," and suddenly powdered-sugary notes float out of the music box Barnabas gave his wife Josette in the eighteenth century, its insufferable ice-cream truck melody inflicting a tinkly soundtrack upon the scene, loud enough to be heard over the metal gate of the mausoleum, which mistakenly creaks before Hoffman even opens it (*Dark Shadows* can't even navigate a flashback without a flub), and of course the gate makes no sound when the occult psychiatrist actually does swing it open

       —my mother struck 31 years later, 1999, in this same room, the day after I tried to explain to her on the phone the editing process for *Strange Prophecies Anew*, my first book of criticism, tried to convey the thrill of galleys and my anxiety I might not find every error and typo before the book went to press later that year, but she didn't understand what galleys were, and now, looking back, I can't imagine why my mother, the daughter of impoverished immigrants whose family survived the Depression feeding off their vegetable garden, her father toiling days in a rubber factory and nights in English classes toward his fatal middle-age heart attack, would know what I meant by "galley":

      Maggie's effort to recall the gated Collins family tomb, to simply "remember a place," casts me back into my family's TV Room, my mother's eventual Stroke Room (forlorn as the Collins tomb but without a squeaky gate), adjacent to the kitchen and perpetually carrying the residual tangy smell of tomato sauce, and I'm swallowed by guilt from our final conversation, Memorial Day, 1999, after my then-wife Shelly and I watched the film *Chicago Cab* on VHS,

and—finally starting to feel comfortable in Chicago after nine months
in the city and wanting to share the marvel that I could attach the
possessive pronoun "my" to a word like "galleys," and remembering,
age six, my mother trying to help me find my first manuscript, which
I'd composed and somehow lost amid scattered doodles and other
first-grade homework (it was a book of jokes appropriated from Dixie
Riddle Cups, plastic drinking cups embossed with gems like, "Why
did Silly Billy throw his clock out the window? He wanted to see time
fly!")—I cut off my mother after my second attempt to explain
"galleys" ("They're like the first part you build of a house, like the
foundation and walls without flooring or paint, and the next round of
galleys will be the house with all the appliances not hooked up yet,"
which she might not have even heard anyway because by 1999 she
was functionally deaf, a malady that runs in the family, her brother
Joe-Joe born deaf and mute, her sisters all outfitted with hearing aids
by their late forties, and I can feel my own ears retreating into murkier
midrange and now I watch TV closed-captioned most of the time) and
asked her brusquely to put my father on the phone and she just took
it—accepted it—like she always did when she couldn't hear what was
being said in a conversation

(which I sometimes experience now, saying "Mm-
hmm" as if I understood all the talk that too often becomes opaque
sound when it reaches my ears, allowing the world to carry on
chatting without me, even though my body is physically present with
the person speaking), and I asked for my father to come on the phone
and we made small talk and, unaware of how cruel it must've
sounded, I complained about my mother's hearing loss as if it were
willful aggression—"I think she can really hear me," I said, "she's just
not listening"—and my father tried to persuade me she actually was
preoccupied by chronic leg pain keeping her awake at night (the blood
clot we didn't know was preparing to rocket up her body into her
brain the next day), and his words nearly prompted me to ask for my
mother back on the phone to apologize—I talked to her that night as if
her inability to understand galleys, a word she'd never heard before,
in a world where she could barely hear anything anymore, was
somehow a burden to *me*—but I didn't, and the next day she had a
stroke in the same room where we watched *Dark Shadows* every day

when I was a child, and we never spoke again, no matter how much I tried in English and Italian for the next two and a half years in the nursing home, the language centers of her brain bereft of words, dead as anything in the Collins family tomb, wiped out by the blood rush of her brain attack the day after I called and tried to explain my precious galleys after watching *Chicago Cab*.

Visiting Chicago's Museum of Contemporary Art, emotionally drained after the saga of my mother and the galleys, I examined every square inch of "Midday Forfit: Feignting Spell II," a Jess Collins collage (no relation to Barnabas), for evidence of *Dark Shadows* influence—Jess and his partner, poet Robert Duncan, watched the show every day—but found nothing vampiric (mere gothic fog over a colonial mansion would've sufficed) in Jess's paste-up of a late-'50s Chevy station wagon, an incongruous, pearl-like orb balanced on its roof and a pair of gemstones functioning as headlights as the car emerged from a lagoon onto a beach of indifferent seals; I froze before the assemblage, mesmerized by the white noise of its deliberate clutter, and, later, watching *Dark Shadows*, I struggled to compose a coda to my story of the Stroke Room until Roger's words to Vicki broke the spell and I remembered the "Midday Forfit" mash-ups my mother and I created every afternoon in 1968, sitting through the interminable romantic entanglements of *Another World* at 3:00 p.m. and *The Edge of Night* at 3:30 p.m., in the Stroke Room, then between 4:00 and 4:30 (right before my father rolled his bicycle up the gravel driveway smelling of sweat, dirt, and rust after another day inspecting steel at "the shop," as he called the factory), we collaged daytime soap melodrama and Collinsport's thanatotic goth: "One day she's perfectly rational and seems to show every hope of recovery," Roger said to Vicki, describing Mrs. Stoddard, "and the next day she's suddenly back to talking about death and mausoleums and being buried alive."

Leap Day 2016 Haiku for David Trinidad

Hair pulled back, pink bow,
Carolyn brooding over
the black telephone.

Returning to the belovèd couplet
to mark my return to Boston,

mid-March weekend visiting Mitch
Evich and Paula Woolley—a friendship

that dates back 30 years, a reminder
we can be closer to the families we choose

than the biological clans that raise us—
first time I've seen Mitch since he was

diagnosed last summer, age 53,
with early-onset Alzheimer's:

my first day back in the city, we walked
from my Copley Square hotel two miles

north to the Institute of Contemporary Art,
where we saw Walid Raad's "Notebook

Volume 38: Already Been in a Lake
of Fire" hanging framed on the walls,

a meticulously archived collection
of magazine cutout images of 145

automobiles—listing and leaning
at different angles from page to page—

each matching the make and model
of vehicles that delivered car bombs

in Lebanon during the country's
civil war, Raad's Arabic text swirling

atop and around the automobiles,
detailing each explosion's blast radius

and casualties, along with the mechanical
specifications of the engines—blown intact

from their cars, which reminded me
of doomed United Airlines Flight 175's

jet engine that tore through the South
Tower on 9/11 before landing at the corner

of Church and Murray Streets, a few blocks
from Ground Zero—but Mitch and I nearly

missed the Raad exhibit altogether,
arriving at the museum a half-hour

before closing, we were lost
for most of the walk, absorbed

in a torrent of conversation,
two writers who simply never

possessed a trustworthy sense
of direction, our lack of compass

now worsened by Mitch's disease
and my total unfamiliarity with

the gentrified South Boston waterfront,
which was nothing but a rotted wharf

and parking lots when I lived here;
Alzheimer's changes everything:

Mitch took us on a tangled, circuitous
route we agreed later was impossible

to chart—we probably covered four
or five miles, but we'll never know

(a GPS map of our wandering would've
resembled coiled Spirograph circles),

Mitch walking so fast I almost had to
jog to keep pace, like we were being

chased, and we were, of course—
by the disease, the renegade

amyloid and tau proteins blocking
cell-to-cell synaptic communication

in his brain ("Will I still be *me*—
my sense of self intact, however

circumscribed—when plaques and tangles
have colonized my brain?" he wrote last

month, an existentially haunting post
on his blog, *The Diminishing Window*);

later, after dinner at Mitch and Paula's,
the three of us walked across the street

to the house of their friend Jay, who
showed me his *Dark Shadows* DVD coffin,

the limited-edition collection that,
like mine, included an autographed

photo of Jonathan Frid, Barnabas himself:
once again, *Dark Shadows* rescued me

from incessant visions of the dead
(like in April 2013, when the show

distracted me from CNN's continuous
coverage of the Boston Marathon bombings),

of what Mitch describes as the "Alzheimer's
end game," the disease's terminal stage;

how consoled I felt earlier today, too,
watching the show in my hotel room

after breakfast, when Adam, the artificial
man, said to Barnabas, "Willie won't tell you,

will he?"—his pun taking me back 65
episodes, to the night Willie Loomis

shivered on the floor of the Collins
family tomb, confessing in voice-over,

"This gives me the willies, even *being*
here"—and how thrilled now, at Jay's,

when he agreed to set up an interview
for me with his friend Gaye, who resides

at Carey Mansion (also known as Seaview
Terrace) in Newport, Rhode Island—

the home ABC used for exterior shots
of the Collinwood estate—such a fan

she deliberately styled her blonde hair after
the witch Angelique's; when she turned 16,

shortly after ABC canceled *Dark Shadows*,
Gaye took a job with the Kansas City

Royals, performing cartwheels along
the basepaths during the fifth inning

of games before sweeping the infield
with a tiny broom she thwacked

the players with, then a few years later
briefly dated Christopher Knight (Peter

Brady from *The Brady Bunch*), completing
an unlikely American pop trifecta—

daytime soaps, baseball, and sitcoms:
Gaye lives in the present moment of

the show's past, renting a room in the *Dark
Shadows* manse, which, from 1975-2009,

was leased as dorm space by Salve
Regina University, whose students

pretty much trashed the place,
Jay said while showing us pictures

he took of himself and Gaye a few
years ago at the mansion, including

shots of the rocks where the waves
famously crash to the tune of a whistling

theremin in the show's opening credits.

A cloudy, windless night, and those who sleep in the Great House of Collinwood do not dream their lives are in danger.

A starless night obscures the walls of Collinwood.

A cold moon illuminates the walls of Collinwood.

While some sleep a quiet sleep in the Great House of Collinwood, others of the Collins family face great danger.

I added an extra sentence (i.e., cheated)
To the previous page—couldn't fight
The alluring banality of the intro teasers—

Watching Episode 590 on the last night
Of the AWP Conference in my dark
LA hotel room after seeing writers

Megan Kaminski, Alan Michael Parker
C. Russell Price, Jaswinder Bolina,
Robyn Schiff, Kristina Marie Darling,

Gaby Williams, Sharon Dolin,
Matthew DeMarco, Hadara Bar-
Nadav, Joe Amato, Susan Schultz,

Andrew Demcak, Kaveh Akbar,
Evan Kleekamp, Dolly Lemke,
Robin Becker, Paige Lewis, Mark

Yakich, Ryan Collins, Siobhán Scarry,
Quraysh Ali Lansana, Amina Cain,
Jen Steele, John Gallaher, Jan Bottiglieri,

Willis Barnstone, Celeste Gainey,
Jan-Henry Gray, James Shea, Maxine
Chernoff, David Hassler, Leif Haven,

Simone Muench, Bill Yarrow, Brandi
Homan, Liz Forsythe, Colleen O'Connor,
Joshua Edwards, Nick Twemlow, Holly

Amos, Kenyatta Rogers, Ben Doller,
Ruth Ellen Kocher, Ralph Hamilton,
Valerie Wallace, and Sandra Doller.

Dr. Hoffman interrupts her *Bride of Frankenstein* experiment to quote French philosopher Henri Bergson on the last day of September 1968; no way I could've known back then, of course, when I saw this episode, age two and suffering constant vampire nightmares, that six weeks before my 50th birthday I'd send a copy of a book (my own, the first volume of this gigantic poem) to Barnabas Collins's physical address—to Jay's friend, Gaye, who lives in the actual mansion ABC used for the show's exterior shots of Collinwood.

"Time passes at Collinwood, and life goes on," Carolyn says, flatlined with ennui, waiting for her goth Godot. A 208-year-old man is plied with speed by a shrink who's in love with him, and a Frankenstein monster broods under a tree: I'd give anything for Edward Albee's human lizards to appear, but his play *Seascape*, featuring talky reptiles Sarah and Leslie, won't premiere until 1975.

Pinching the top of a white chessboard queen with this thumb and forefinger, Nicholas Blair lectures Adam on his talent for raising the dead.

"I won't disturb her rest for long," says Professor Stokes to Adam, who counters: "You *will not* disturb her rest at all" (a perfectly iambic exchange bisected by a bacchius—thank you, Nate Breitling, on the second anniversary of your death, for this lyric gift from beyond).

After 45 episodes of Dr. Hoffman's false starts and palsied reaction shots—flailing over knobs and levers and electronic curios in her basement laboratory lit by candles perched in sconces—Adam's Bride of Frankenstein, predictably named Eve, finally comes to life: strapped to Hoffman's operating table, entering this world wearing a black evening dress and black velvet pumps (ABC forced heels on Eve's insensate feet before they'd even walked the earth, damning her to a life of nerve damage, ingrown toenails, bunions, and hammertoes without first giving her a chance to learn how to get around in bare feet or flats), caked in foundation and blush, eyes hooded by enormous lashes that flap wildly as she opens them, like a socialite startled by her butler from an afternoon nap—a chic, cosmopolitan artificial woman who, despite being manufactured from decomposing body parts, looks more like Helen Gurley Brown than Elsa Lanchester, the original Bride of Frankenstein, whose iconic, gray-haired lightning streak coiffed her conical mane into an electrical beehive; later, after running her long fingers through her hair and accidentally sliding her wig out of place, Eve launches into an existential soliloquy that could be an outtake from George Oppen's *Of Being Numerous* ("There are things / We live among," Oppen writes, "'and to see them / Is to know ourselves'"), published this same year, 1968, four months before Eve awakens in Hoffman's laboratory: "How could I have not lived until now," Eve says, awestruck and surprised, like the speaker of nearly every Oppen poem, by her direct perception of the simple things of this world, "I'm fully grown. I know you are men. She's a woman. I know this is a basement. And I know all these things."

His throat pinched by a candy cane-
striped bow tie, Professor Stokes repeats
his exact words from the end of yesterday's
episode—"Adam, that woman upstairs
is the reincarnation of the most evil woman
who was ever born"—sending a message
to my mother, watching with her two-year-old
insomniac son, that although the women's movement
was radically changing her life (the first national
women's liberation conference would be held
a month later, Thanksgiving, 1968, in Lake Villa,
Illinois), she should harbor no illusion
that the glamorous Bride of Frankenstein who just
rose from the Old House basement operating table
might become the show's first major female character
not kidnapped by a vampire,
not a witch who curses a man to vampirism
after coercing him into marrying her,
not strangled by the man she doomed
to vampirism when she was a witch,
not killed by a witchfinder then resurrected
by a warlock, not stalked in a graveyard
by a vampire, or not bitten by her 208-year-old
vampire cousin.
   Little David, the psychic child,
reappears after a 57-episode absence, reclining
in a copper velour sweater and brown corduroy
pencil pants in Adam's secret bedroom hovel,
while Adam is holed up at the House by the Sea
with his newly hatched Bride of Frankenstein,
their nascent romance causing Carolyn's
bottom lip to quiver in close-up—
   I'm watching
Dark Shadows in New York for the first time,
staying with Liz at the Washington Square Hotel,
just three miles from where the show was taped
at ABC Studios on the Upper West Side,

and I'm worried that the first representations
of love and romance I witnessed as a boy
(beyond the cheek-pecks my father routinely
bestowed upon my mother when he got home
from work) actually were the most demented
introductions to human intimacy a toddler
might experience sitting in front of a TV set
in the late 1960s: Carolyn is jealous of an artificial man,
stitched together from the body parts of corpses,
who ran off with a woman also quilted from
the dead, which should come as no surprise,
since necromania runs in the Collins family —
her 208-year-old cousin once kidnapped
Maggie Evans, whose vulnerable jugular
throbbed in time with mine (we both were
vampire prey, as far as I was concerned),
and locked her in his basement dungeon
when she refused to become his vampire-lover,
his twentieth-century Josette, who leaped to her
death from Widows' Hill in 1796 to escape
the witch Angelique, who later cast a spell
on her own husband, Barnabas, turning him
into a vampire after he shot her with a pistol
in the Old House parlor: by the time I was two
years old, straddling the cusp between
toddler-talk and language, *Dark Shadows*
already had prepared me for my Catholic
childhood, teaching that it wasn't unusual to desire
(or be desired by) inanimate flesh and that romance
always ends with someone getting punished
for love.

       Stage lights glaring off his bear-claw
comb-over, Barnabas realizes he can't keep
Maggie, whose dad was killed by Angelique
81 episodes ago, locked up in the mausoleum forever —
the women in my mother's soaps rattled the yoke
of the father, but it choked them as soon as they
tried to strike out on their own (except for

minidresses and psychedelic, shawl-collared
blazers, you wouldn't know it's 1968 in Collinsport,
that a month before today's episode, the term
"bra-burning feminist" would be created
by reporters covering a protest of the Miss America
pageant by the New York Radical Women;
no bras were actually burned—
                              they threw bras,
mops, girdles, pots and pans, and copies of *Playboy*
into a large trash can which they planned
to set ablaze, but the Atlantic City boardwalk
police wouldn't let them start the fire).
Bonus sentence from the next episode,
the show's 600th: "You think of me as a piece
of property, as something you own,"
Eve says to Adam—in a year of worldwide
social and political revolution, ABC decided
the show's first major feminist statement
should be uttered by an artificial woman
constructed from the grave-robbed flesh
of the dead—"a woman doesn't like to be
thought of in those terms."

Professor Stokes commemorates Episode 600 calling for yet another *Dark Shadows* séance, reminding me how frustrated I was, as a child, that my parents, unlike the adults on the show, did *not* routinely conduct late-night séances (of course, they didn't need to lock their fingers around a circular table and summon the spirits of the dead, since a vampire lived inside the walls of their house, watching for when their son let down his guard and relaxed his hunched shoulders and fell asleep).

Things I did on my 50th birthday: ate toast, prunes, and soy bacon for breakfast, with three espresso cups of Arabic coffee; answered two emails from my college's study abroad coordinator about an incendiary student conflict that erupted during this summer's Prague program (I'm chair of our department for one more year, and I've come to accept that emails like these can arrive on my half-century birthday); attended Sunday service at the Chicago Zen Buddhist Temple; worked on the "candy cane-striped bow tie" segment of this book; ripped Sleater-Kinney's *Dig Me Out* and Black Sabbath's *Live in Hammersmith* (1978 bootleg) to iTunes; took a three-mile walk along the lakefront with Liz, where we discussed our upcoming visit to Israel—she was awarded a research grant, and I'm tagging along—especially how we'd get from Tel Aviv to East Jerusalem on the third day of the trip; after the walk, sat on the grass at Loyola Park, three blocks from our apartment, and watched The Pratt Cattz, a local jazz band led by a keyboardist who used to play with Miles Davis and Tony Williams; ate birthday dinner at Calo's restaurant (Liz: Penne Pasta with Pesto; me: Farfalle Pomodoro della Verdura); called Verizon after dinner—the operator's name was Angelique ("Hello, my name is Angelique," she said, "how can I help you?" and I thought, *Oh, my, you already have*)—and added an international calling plan for the Middle East; watched *Dark Shadows* (Adam too busy fending off an evil spirit choking him to notice that Nicholas seemed to be wearing Barnabas's psychedelic, Pre-Raphaelite smoking jacket); before going to bed, put on the last five minutes of Game 7 of the NBA Finals (Cleveland Cavaliers beat the Golden State Warriors, the city's first major professional sports championship in 52 years).

"Happy 50th Anniversary of the first broadcast
of *Dark Shadows*," I write in my Moleskine
on 6/24/16, "I'm five days older than the show itself";
next week I'll remember the first episode
actually was broadcast 6/27/66, but tonight
I'm excited by the (mistaken) belief that I'm
commemorating the show's golden anniversary:
Nicholas Blair (wearing what looks suspiciously
like Barnabas's psychedelic, Pre-Raphaelite
smoking jacket for the second episode in a row)
spies on Jeff Clark through an enchanted
wall mirror in the House by the Sea—
Clark asleep in his bed, Angelique leaning
over his neck, fangs bared between her puffy
dimples, an image that fed my childhood belief
that the mirrors in my grandmother's home
functioned, like Blair's, as metaphysical conduits,
                    that ghosts of the recently dead
roamed her second floor and snooped on me—
sometimes through mirror glass, but often
from behind the eyes of three devotional
Jesus portraits in the hallway I refused
to make eye contact with (my recollections
of the paintings are blurry, since I tried so hard
not to see—or be seen by—them as a child,
but I'm sure that one of the portraits was
Warner Sallman's iconic *Head of Christ*);
much later, age 12, I still believed
my grandmother's upstairs hallway
and bedrooms housed warlock Jesus
surveillance operatives, and I was petrified
these ghosts of the upper floor reported
my thoughts to guardian angels who were
prepared to abandon me (in my unforgiving
cosmology, your angels could make
themselves vanish if they determined
you'd become irredeemable) for indiscretions
like mocking the sacred Nicene Creed,

the bedrock profession of Catholic faith
we recited in mass every week:
          "We believe in one Lord, Jesus Christ,
the only Son of God," the Creed begins—
its required mystical obedience alienating me
from the start, and to keep myself awake
in church I often substituted Patty Hearst,
Batgirl, and Wendy O. Williams
(she was the Holy Ghost, of course)
for the Trinity, saying their names
under my breath, or I imagined my heart
battered by a halftone-dotted, three-person'd god
collaged from interchangeable members
of the Justice League of America;
but the sonic tumble of the next lines actually
hooked me—"eternally begotten of the Father, /
God from God, Light from Light, / true God
from true God, / begotten, not made, / one in Being
with the Father"—they mesmerized me
a decade after first watching *Dark Shadows*
with my mother, the sound of the words obscuring
their sense—no surprise my first poetry obsession
was Dylan Thomas's gorgeously incomprehensible
(for me, as a teenager) language and syntax,
and I could almost believe Thomas wrote
those lines from the Nicene Creed during another
of his dozen-shot whiskey benders (I stole Thomas's
Collected Poems from the high school library—
confession: it still sits among my books at home
—and I'd walk up to friends at their lockers,
reciting, "Altarwise by owl-light in the half-way
house / The gentleman lay graveward with his furies,"
followed by what I felt was a better third line,
"Begotten, not made, one in Being with the Father")—
          the old-world southern Italian matriarchal
Catholicism my grandmother passed down
to my mother, a paganism she once called
"voodoo Catholicism," didn't need the Church

to teach magic and ethics and morals,
and it resembled Dylan Thomas's bacchanalian
rage for disorder more than it did the Catholic
pledge of allegiance the Church fathers composed
for us at Nicea, which, I've just realized
as I write this, is another reason to cite
when friends ask why I was allowed to watch
Dark Shadows every day with my mother
despite my incessant nightmares:
the show substituted for the ancestral
supernaturalism of Montenero, her family's
tiny village built into the hills southeast of Rome,
and it offered a chance to share the uncanny
with her two-year-old son in the living room
of her tiny home in Pennsylvania—
later, cupping her palm to my forehead
when I crawled into my parents' bed
after a nightmare, a palm at the end of my mind,
beyond the last thought, on the edge of space,
my shoulders hunched to ward off a vampire.

Watching *Dark Shadows* with Liz in Tel Aviv, 6/27/16, the (real) 50th anniversary of the show's first broadcast: Mrs. Stoddard returns from a 25-episode absence in full-throttle necromania, proudly showing off a cheap, cardboard-cutout scale model mausoleum she commissioned an architect to build—the word "STODDARD" embossed in all caps above the entrance arch, adding a warm, personal touch to the tomb she prefers to be buried alive in; "It's a dollhouse of a mausoleum," Liz says, looking beyond my laptop, out the hotel room's giant rectangular window onto the Mediterranean Sea, where, last night, drenched in humidity, we watched the pinprick red sun set 24 hours after we'd been whisked to O'Hare from our apartment in Rogers Park, the far North Side of Chicago, by an Uber driver listening to auto-tuned pop music (didn't recognize any of the artists, their voices squeezed by software into one narrow, nasal frequency range), and 13 hours after we arrived in New York for our connecting flight with El Al, when Liz, worried about returning to Israel, her home for five years in the mid-'90s—fearing it's changed enormously since then (I experience similar anxiety every time I return to Boston, one of the most important cities of my imagination)—concluded we were doomed to lose our luggage: "The El Al agent I spoke to on the phone told me we'd have to meet someone for an extra security check after we got to New York," she said to the agent at our JFK departure gate, "and we'd have to be matched to our bags," her voice rising at the end of every phrase, a familiar post-9/11 passive inflection that signals to airline personnel you'll be a submissive passenger, her words trying to make themselves invisible as soon as they left her mouth (the gate agent, of course, studying her for any suspicious deviation from the passive voice), "but I called JetBlue three times, and *they* kept saying our bags are checked straight through from New York to Tel Aviv," she continued, sidling a little too close to the gate agent trained to examine her passport for evidence of nefarious intent—the whole scene reminding me of Episode 413, when Vicki couldn't stop herself from predicting Ghost Girl's death, even though she was trying to convince Collinsport she wasn't a witch— "El Al said we have to check them at the gate, but we already checked our bags in Chicago," she added, "and JetBlue, which we flew from Chicago, is pretty clear we'll meet our bags in Tel Aviv," at which point Liz's shift back to active voice prompted the agent to look up at her and exhale: "Do what El Al tells you," he said, "and have a nice flight."

Three days later in Jerusalem, after a long walk in the Old City, guessing which paving stones were 2,000 years old and which were made to look this way after 1967—a day Liz discovered to her distress that the Old City's Jaffa Gate is now connected to Mamilla Mall (we can shop at The Gap, The North Face, American Eagle, and Timberland before taking a stroll on ancient paving stones in a walled sector of a colonized city) and the new Simon Wiesenthal Museum of Tolerance is being constructed atop a 900-year-old Muslim cemetery (also named Mamilla)—Dr. Hoffman jumps out of bed screaming from a nightmare, each squeal so awkward that her discomfort as a performer almost feels deliberate (it's not, she's just a terrible actor), an extravagantly dissonant symphony of overacting rivaled only by Divine's homicidal tantrum in the *Female Trouble* nightclub scene, right before she pulls out a pistol and mows down her audience ("Thank you from the bottom of my black little heart," she shrieks, "I'm so fucking beautiful I can't stand it myself! Now, everybody freeze! Who wants to be famous? Who wants to *die* for art?").

"The man isn't aware that he knows what we know about him," Barnabas says of Nicholas Blair, accidentally transforming his flubbed line into a surveillance-state koan on 10/18/68, the day the U.S. Olympic Committee suspends Tommie Smith and John Carlos for raising their black-gloved fists in a Black Power salute from the victory podium when they received their gold (Smith) and bronze (Carlos) medals—if my mother, my first political mentor, were alive today, 7/20/16, her 90th birthday, she'd appreciate their black fists superimposed on goth-white Collinsport—the suspension announced at 3:30 p.m. in Mexico City (as the credits rolled on Episode 605) in a statement that Douglas F. Roby, president of the U.S. Olympic Committee, read before the Men's 400-Meter track-and-field final to athletes Lee Evans, Larry James, and Ron Freeman, who went out straightaway and swept the 400-Meter, taking the gold, silver, and bronze respectively, the *New York Times* describing them as "black power advocates," but reassuring readers these particular black men were no threat: "On arriving at the victory platform and on leaving it, they did raise clenched fists," reporter Joseph M. Sheehan observes, "but they were smiling and apparently not defiant as they did so."

Barnabas sneaks into Eve's bedroom in the middle of the night, her window opened onto the grounds of Collinwood, the bed's ice-blue, embroidered canopy rustling in the breeze, a gauzy scene in the notorious House by the Sea; Barnabas's tiptoed crouch, Inverness cape draped over his shoulders, wolf's-head cane in hand, evokes yet another recurring childhood nightmare—he's leaning over my bed, examining me like a specimen in a lab, and I'm petrified, frozen by sleep paralysis (sounds like stagehands are playing table tennis off camera later in the episode—kitsch incongruity that would've soothed my vampire fears as a child, if only I'd known, age two, what a blooper was—but my hearing is on the decline, and the staccato pops could easily be stagehands' coughs, not ping-pong balls getting smacked around).

~

Occult, woo-pitching flurry in Collinsport tonight, triggered no doubt by the amorous sitar drone coming from the Blue Whale jukebox (no more Sesame Street bepop at the bar; it's 1968 and everyone knows George Harrison has been taking sitar lessons from Ravi Shankar for over a year now): to shake Joe's heartbroken attachment to her, the vampire Angelique leads him to Nicholas Blair's magic mirror, where, after the two see the reflection of a stagehand rolling a blue chroma-key screen behind Joe's head, they watch Nicholas and Maggie, Joe's ex-girlfriend, dawdling by Maggie's door after their date, Nicholas confessing his love before leaning into Maggie for a motionless smooch (once again, a *Dark Shadows* kiss comes off like an awkward hug), prompting Joe—the only star-crossed Romeo in daytime soap history to be dumped by both a vampire and a woman kidnapped by a vampire—to pick up a letter opener and press it against his stomach: "If you only knew how much you bore me," Angelique says, facing away from Joe as he plunges the letter opener into his body.

With Liz and Gene Kannenberg at a throwback screening of *Planet of the Apes*—released in 1968, six months before Maggie's overwrought Episode 608 introduction, "One man has discovered that both sacred *and* profane love can leave you completely alone" (*Dark Shadows*, the Joy Division of daytime TV)—first time I've seen this film on the big screen since 1974, age eight, a *Planet of the Apes* marathon (all five movies, all day) at the Warner Theatre, a plush art deco cinema in Erie, Pennsylvania, where I begged my brother Carmen to take me with him and our two cousins (he relented only because my parents forced him to), and during the intermission between the third and fourth films—*Escape from the Planet of the Apes* and *Conquest of the Planet of the Apes*—I went to the men's room with them and, self-conscious that I didn't know how to use a urinal, watched how my brother walked up to an empty one and imitated him, pulling my penis through the fly hole in my underwear, but I didn't adequately maneuver it from the flap, and for some reason didn't understand you must point your penis at the urinal, causing me to streak my underwear and jeans with my stream; I felt lucky no one saw it, assumed I'd gotten away with my accident, until I felt a huge damp spot on the right inner thigh of my jeans as the fourth movie began, and by the end of *Conquest of the Planet of the Apes*, the odor had become inescapable, at which point I noticed my brother watching the movie turned three-quarters away from me—he endured it and never said a word, even though he must've realized his reward for taking me to a five-movie marathon was the acrid smell of urine for the last two films (three hours of screen time, plus intermission).

Adam and Eve trade bewildered soliloquies to celebrate my 400th episode, flirting like two graduate students learning to do things with words: "Strange, they just named the season for the fact that the leaves *fall* from the trees," Adam says, adding, "that doesn't seem possible—they certainly would have chosen a more complicated name," prompting Eve to stare off camera, her face pinched, concentrating: "Why do I remember that sometimes the trees have no leaves at all," she intones, "and at other times the leaves are green?"

Early September in Chicago, the city drowsing Keatsian into autumn, each day palpably shorter and the cicadas finally quiet, my first sidewalk leaf-fall sighting this week, a reminder we'll be living in bare-tree radio silence by Thanksgiving—not soon enough for Mrs. Stoddard, consumed by the fantasy she'll wake one day in a casket locked in a tomb with the word "STODDARD" carved into its entryway arch ("Perhaps if you keep me busy enough, I can even convince myself that I'll be alive on your wedding day," she says after Vicki announces her engagement to Jeff Clark).

Nicholas Blair snuffs a candle with his palm.

Harry doesn't understand why he's succumbed
to Nicholas, and I don't understand how one character
could jam so much exposition into a stuttering, 44-
second (timed on my stopwatch) voice-over: "I—I wish
I could keep the clock from striking—I don't want to
leave this house—I don't *want* to go [like Morrissey]
back to the Old House—I don't want to put this poison
in that bottle of medicine, but I gotta do it—
       [pause DVD, distracted by the sight
of Harry's mother, Mrs. Johnson, making her first
appearance after a 42-episode absence]—
              I gotta do
everything Nicholas Blair tells me to do—I don't
understand why—I—I just know I *have* to obey him—
I—I have to go now—I don't want to, but I have to."
            "She sounds psychotic,"
Liz says after listening to Dr. Hoffman's droning
introduction to Episode 613—"The hour of dawn
lingers far out at sea beyond the cliffs of Collinwood, as
though reluctant to bring the light of day to the land
around the ancient house"—four hours after I promised
her over iced coffee and ginger tea at Ellipsis
Coffeehouse that I'd put her in the poem again if she
watched *Dark Shadows* with me tonight ("It *has* been a
while," she said, reaching for her tea).
         Halloween, 1968, Joe strangles
Barnabas, as he did in the final scene of the previous
episode, but this time we're spared a close-up of
Barnabas's decrepit upper molars.

His fingers wrapped in a decadent grip around the looped handle of his wolf's-head cane (black onyx ring on right pointer finger), Barnabas Collins slaps my childhood bedroom window with an autocratic snap of the wrist, shattering the glass, at which point my memory of this recurring dream wavers, a glitch effect, the dreamspace fractured in sheared, horizontal pieces, like images from a broken analog television, as I toggle between my 1968 vampire nightmares and Episode 615 tonight, the 15th anniversary of 9/11: the camera zooms on Barnabas's hand, his fingers gripping Joe Haskell's glass medicine vial, the close-up resurrecting my childhood fear that I'd wake up in the middle of the night without my shoulders hunched and the last thing I'd ever see would be his right hand—elliptical onyx surrounded by gold band (the wounding detail of my *Dark Shadows* nightmares)—as it brushed away my collar to expose my bare neck and jugular, a fear that triggers a body memory of the excruciating bottom-right-molar throb that kept me awake the Friday before the attacks, that by the next weekend, one day after the airports opened again, required an emergency root canal: the endodontist couldn't numb me, and she had no choice but to drop the anesthetic directly on my inflamed nerve, shocking pain that flashed just long enough for me to remember I was terrified her office was in a high-rise (two weeks later, I stopped meditating—didn't for more than a year—because of phantom tooth pain and every time I sat on my cushion I put myself into those planes).

Have you given Joe the medicine? From now on, it's going to be all smiles and cheer; they'll fill the room with flowers and candles.

If you marry Jeff Clark, it will be the most tragic mistake of your life. I want you to get Barnabas back to the Old House tonight—I want you to leave him there, and I want you to stay away from him.

We'll have our nights, both of us, and our days will be spent in coffins.

Get me the stake
      and the mallet—
I still have blood plasma
      downstairs,
from the experiment—

close the drapes—
      go to Collinwood,
go to *my* room and use
      the phone—
don't use any other
      phone and don't
let anyone see you—

Let me help you, or you can forget about Jeff Clark, because he doesn't want you and he isn't going to want you—not unless you can prove beyond any doubt that he really is Peter Bradford.

Take it out of this house, take it far into the woods, as far as you can, and burn it, burn every page of it. You agree so easily, I don't trust you at all.

If I let you read, will you go away and leave me alone for the rest of my life?

You take my advice—start a life that'll be real.

> Go back to the house
>   as if nothing happened,
> and when Nicholas
>   tells you Eve is dead,
> you must pretend
>   to be so shocked—
> stricken with grief—
>   you'll do anything
> he wants you to do.

I call out all the dark creatures of nature to summon you to me. You will infuse the body with a new life force and bring it alive again, and you'll have all day tomorrow to prepare. Take the stone and drop it in the cup. If you want tomorrow to happen, you better meet me tonight.

Lock me in here, and if you happen to hear noises during the night—I sometimes move around and act out when I'm writing, it kind of gets me into it—don't pay any attention to anything.

Watching the Thanksgiving Eve 1968 episode five days before Thanksgiving 2016 and 11 days after Donald Trump's election—good night from the end of the American experiment, the KKK just announced a December 3 victory rally and the rest of us have become a nation of dissidents—Maggie strapped to one of Dr. Hoffman's operating tables wearing a translucent yellow chiffon nightgown, screaming as Barnabas flips a wall lever that triggers steampunk static and submarine sonar pings, followed by an inexplicable close-up of a red orb that looks more like a traffic signal than a functioning component of a mad-scientist laboratory; Hoffman's oscilloscope screen is stuck in a looping green flat line, the machine simply not equipped to measure this kind of pandemonium, Maggie screeching so loudly amid the static and pings I'm afraid my downstairs neighbors will complain, a racket worsened when Hoffman quotes a line from Ralph Hodgson's poem, "Eve," as she looks down upon ABC's Eve, the show's artificial woman, coming to life with a rise of her left arm on the operating table next to Maggie's ("'Poor motherless Eve,'" Hoffman exclaims, adding pedantically, "there's a poem about that"); later in the scene, Sean Dhu Sullivan, directing his final *Dark Shadows* episode, adds to the bedlam with a shot of Eve suddenly decomposed—brought back to life and destroyed again over a three-and-a-half-minute span (timed on my stopwatch)—her skeleton still buckled to the operating table but her clothes partially pulled away, exposing the browned bones of her rib cage and suggesting that the top half of her black evening gown somehow disintegrated along with her body, after which Hoffman leads Maggie away from the clatter of the operating theater, their footsteps a chorus of squishing and crackling, like they're walking on peanut shells—a feast of dissonant rot for my mother and me the day before the third Thanksgiving of my life.

2.

Night over the Great House of Collinwood. Night filled with unexplained acts.

The dread vampire of my childhood nightmares looks through the barred window of the Old House cellar door and picks his nose with his onyx ring finger, shamelessly flicking away the booger as if bored by the unremitting shrieks of Victoria Winters, who's strapped to a basement operating table and played by Betsy Durkin for the third consecutive episode since the departure of Alexandra Moltke, who left *Dark Shadows* to give birth to her son, Adam—born 6/27/69, the third anniversary of the show's premiere, but probably not named after the show's artificial man-child—and who later became Claus von Bülow's lover: prosecutors in von Bülow's attempted-murder trial claimed his love for Moltke led him to inject Sunny, his wife, with an overdose of insulin, sending her into a permanent vegetative state for the final 28 years of her life.

"I'm convinced this place is haunted," says occult detective Professor Stokes on the evening of the 2016 winter solstice, the first episode I've watched since the all-day fast and bowel cleanse 10 days ago for my first colonoscopy (Barnabas caught picking his nose at sunset the afternoon of my fast; a half-hour later I drank the magic laxative potion that launched my excremental purge, a fitting metaphor these dark days before the inauguration, the U.S. gutted from the inside by Donald Trump, whose national security advisor, General Michael Flynn, conferred three days ago with neo-Nazi Heinz-Christian Strache, leader of Austria's Freedom Party, which was created after World War II as a postwar haven for former Nazis), "but in all my reading," Stokes continues, "I've never encountered a ghost who used the telephone."

Our November ritual: every night
before dinner I'd wash my hands

while Liz, sitting at the kitchen table,
chose a spot on her stomach just

far enough from the previous
day's injection to prevent swelling;

I daubed the area with an alcohol
swab, swiping it across her skin

long enough to give her time to take
a breath and look away before

I inserted the needle, which I did
immediately, pushing the plunger

with my thumb until I'd injected
all the drug from the vial, 40 mg

of Lovenox, shooting the anti-
coagulant into her stomach each

night to prevent blood clots from
developing after her surgery;

and now, the last days of December,
seven weeks past Liz's election-day

hysterectomy—three ping-pong-ball-
sized tumors had been pushing out

of her uterus, distending her the size
of a woman sixteen weeks pregnant,

the surgeon wrote in her post-
operative report—the two of us

visiting Michael and Trish in San Diego,
watching *Dark Shadows* in our room

at the Sheraton, late-afternoon
sunlight slipping over the mountain

outside our balcony: put down
the phone, Vicki, it's too late to call

Prof. Stokes, director Lela Swift
already is shooting gargly-voiced

Jeff Clark in chroma-key, flailing his
arms, shrinking as he disappears

back into 1795; instead of growing
old and dying outright, the residents

of Collinwood are vanishing into
ceaselessly flowing past lives,

summoned by whatever century
requires their presence in its narrative

stream, suggesting to two-year-old
viewers watching on 12/3/68 with

their mothers that, as an alternative
to dying, some people simply don

period costumes while set designers
replace the soundstage props;

if I live long enough to navigate
this impossible object of a poem

into my elder years, I'll need to find
a way to write about aging without

wishing all the old things were new —
as recently as my early thirties, I believed

I'd resist the rickety breakdowns
of old age through sheer force of will,

a ludicrous faith I didn't question until
New Year's Day, 1999, age 32, stuck

inside during Chicago's worst blizzard
in three decades, the day my 15-year-old

amplifier, cassette deck, and speakers
croaked all at once; when it became

clear they were too old to be saved,
I realized my body was no more or less

flimsy than my audio system, an insight
I promptly ignored (the metaphor was

banal, but it terrified me, all the same)
until my mother's stroke four months later

—no exertion of her will, no stubborn
refusal to believe the body is fragile,

could stop a blood clot from racing up
her leg, into her brain: I'm embarrassed

to admit I needed the planned obso-
lescence of an audio appliance before

I could consider that breaking down
is actually the body's modus operandi;

as this vampire soap opera poem
and I grow old in each other, I can't

ignore that no matter how good
I feel today (next to Liz on the bed,

my laptop between us, the Southern
California sun casting a sepia glow

through the sliding doors of the room
we'll inhabit for another three days,

pausing the DVD to draft this sentence
in my Moleskine notebook), I'll be too

damaged to watch *Dark Shadows*, let alone
write about it, if I don't take three pills

every morning for my enlarged prostate,
one of which delivers a blast of estrogen

to counteract the excess testosterone
my body has produced so many

years it's made me bald and swelled
my prostate so large I'd piss every

half hour if not for the two other pills
I take to relax my bladder: writing about

my prescriptions makes me worry that
if I manage to cheat death long enough

to finish this poem's 1,225th sentence, I can't
allow my experiment in autobiography

to lapse into a versified pharmacological
profile, especially considering how alien

my father's collection of pill bottles once
seemed, his meds for shoulder arthritis,

high cholesterol, prostate cancer,
high blood pressure, and anxiety

lined up in formation on the kitchen
shelf above the toaster—confession,

I claimed the Valium after he died in 2009,
pocketing the pills the weekend of my

43rd birthday as I cleaned my childhood
home of his possessions before the house

was put on the market, snatched them
before anyone else in my family could get

their hands on the bottle (those pills
my father's gift from the beyond

that first summer without parents).

Dr. Hoffman hands out sedatives like candy, which makes me jealous, my dead father's Valium long gone, unable to sleep at night, 11 days into Trump's presidency and worried about how totalitarianism will change me ("Write a list of things you would never believe," journalist Sarah Kendzior advises, "because it is possible that in the next year, you will either believe them or be forced to say you believe them"): more pills for Vicki, who claims Jeff Clark's spectral hand reached out from 1795 and touched her cheek in 1968, the likely origin of my childhood fear that a ghost would physically touch me, not just manifest in wisp or apparition but actually announce itself in tactile form, press itself against me from the spirit world—my toddler goth anxieties haunting the first episode I've watched since the inauguration ("Write your biography, write down your memories, because if you do not do it now, you may forget," says Kendzior), Collinsport's first werewolf appearing the same night Trump fires his acting attorney general for refusing to enforce his executive order banning travelers from Iran, Iraq, Syria, Sudan, Libya, Yemen, and Somalia—shades of Richard Nixon's 1973 Saturday Night Massacre, when the country's top two Justice Department officials resigned rather than follow Nixon's order to fire the special prosecutor investigating him (Kendzior: "Write a list of things you would never do, because it is possible that in the next year you will do them")— Trump splitting up families who, like Germans on the wrong side of the Berlin Wall when the border was closed overnight in 1961, had the simple bad luck to be traveling abroad when his executive order was signed.

"Sit quietly, the sedative will work very quickly," Dr. Hoffman says to Mrs. Stoddard, while a new character, rheumy-eyed Little Orphan Amy, prepubescent runaway from Windcliff Sanitarium, explores the abandoned West Wing of the Great House with Little David, the psychic child, summoning the ghost of Quentin Collins on a broken nineteenth-century telephone under a stringy mozzarella-cobweb canopy—unaware that her brother, Chris Jennings, roams Collinsport covered in fur and growling. Amy and David hunched over the ancient telephone, its wires hanging loose, their direct line to the restive dead of Collinsport: yes, Henry James, if one psychic child gave my nightmares a turn of the screw, then "two children gave two turns."

"Don't tell me it was a dream again, because I wasn't asleep at all"—don't waste your breath, Little Orphan Amy, this explanation never convinced my parents that Barnabas Collins smashed my bedroom window with his wolf's-head cane, and it's not about to persuade Vicki you saw a vision of your werewolf brother alone in the woods sobbing beneath the moon.

Like the fuzzy blue ghost-orb that just floated into Vicki's bedroom and stopped the wristwatch Jeff Clark gave her before he vanished into 1795, I drift through long stretches of each day, barely absorbing each new derangement before the next, even more inexplicable one occurs (Trump bans immigrants, threatens judges, accuses Barack Obama and the British government of colluding to wiretap his offices, tweets diatribes about Academy Award winners, walks around the White House in his bathrobe fuming that *Saturday Night Live* chose a woman to play his press secretary): today at a Dean's Council meeting, I met our new Vice President of

Global Education (I've stopped counting how many vice presidents we've added at my college the past two years), who grew up in Argentina, and all I wanted to do was pick his brain about how he survived the Argentinian dirty war of the 1970s without being "disappeared"—not garden-variety paranoia, but a plea for advice on how to live as a citizen-hostage in a totalitarian state; instead of paying attention to his PowerPoint slides on our study abroad programs, I played the Anne Frank Game, taught to me by Liz, who, as a ten-year-old, hid sobbing in the basement of her home because the National Socialist Party of America was about to march in Skokie: if this were an attic in Amsterdam in 1942, who among the dean and the new vice president and my fellow chairs from every department in the School of Liberal Arts and Sciences would hide me—and who would snitch to the Gestapo?

"I have some sleeping pills if you want to try one," Roger says to Carolyn, who's agitated after a traumatic séance and backlit by strobe flashes synced to an endless loop of thundercracks, another sedative-popping night of low-budget special effects in Collinsport. The erotic strings of "Shadows of the Night (Quentin's Theme)" arise from the thunderstorm, prompting Little David, the psychic child, to affirm his heteronormative bona fides—no, Amy, he doesn't want to play dress-up with clothes his ancestors once wore: a waltz nominated for a 1969 Grammy, "Quentin's Theme," as the song came to be known, was released 6/27/69 as part of a *Dark Shadows* soundtrack album, with lyrics penned by Charles Randolph Grean, a version that would spend 11 weeks on Billboard's Top 100 the summer of '69 and transform Quentin into the show's bad-boy werewolf dreamboat; the tune was covered almost immediately as a seven-inch single (released 8/15/69, less than a week after the Tate-LaBianca murders) by French actress and pop star Claudine Longet, who, eight years later, 1977, would be convicted of misdemeanor negligent homicide in the death of her boyfriend, former Olympic skier Spider Sabich, after a trial in which Longet claimed Sabich was demonstrating how to use his gun when it accidentally discharged (autopsy report suggested he was bent over, facing away, and at least six feet from Longet in the bathroom when the gun was fired), Sabich killed just two years after Longet's divorce from bland, easy-listening crooner Andy Williams, who also cashed in on the song, recording his own cover version in 1969, two months after Longet's (for the album *Get Together with Andy Williams*) and 10 months after tonight's episode, broadcast 12/12/68, when the song made its *Dark Shadows* debut as a scratchy Victrola recording that emanated from inside the walls of the abandoned West Wing, a spectral reminder that the ghost of Quentin Collins inhabited the inside of the inside of the Great House—which made absolute sense to me, age two, hunching my shoulders before going to sleep every night because, like Quentin, Barnabas Collins also lived inside the walls of other people's homes. A third turn of the barely coherent narrative screw: after a bad dream, Little Orphan Amy lies about watching the sun rise (*tomorrow, tomorrow*) with David so that 208-year-old Barnabas won't discover that the two enchanted children just broke into his home to steal a nineteenth-century wooden cradle for a ghost baby, as instructed by their spirit guide, Quentin, who haunts the children through a disconnected antique telephone with severed wires flopping from its base.

Seventy-one years rotted and still clad in the burgundy sweater-vest and tie he was wearing when he died, Quentin's desiccated skeleton reclines in a chair next to the mantel inside the walls of the abandoned West Wing of the Great House ("Quentin's Theme" playing on the Victrola, of course), while a few feet away, his mute ghost stands before Little David and Little Orphan Amy—slathered in blush and ghoulish eyeliner, his jaw framed by massive mutton chops— three hours after my first ever reading in New York, hosted by Charles North at Pace University (the start of a mini tour for Book 2 of this poem, *Inside the Walls of My Own House*), my laptop perched between my knees on the bed at the Washington Square Hotel, pausing Episode 646—freeze-frame, Quentin's inscrutable face—to read a text message just received from Michael Trigilio: "We were in NYC exactly one year ago for my screening at Anthology Film Archives, and there's no better visit than when the city has invited you—feels like golden wind."

"My family has made the two of us very unhappy—they must be made to realize that," David said to Amy after the Pace reading last week, "they must pay for what they've done to us" (paused the DVD that night, texted a clip of the scene to David Trinidad, who replied, "Little David's going to grow up to be a confessional poet!"), and six days later, still possessed by Quentin—an episode I'll watch in Chicago with lights off and shades drawn on the witch holiday Walpurgisnacht—Little David will booby-trap the carpeted stairs in the Great House foyer so that his father, Roger, might trip and break his neck (does it count as "Oedipal" if the son is a psychic child compelled by a 71-year-old ghost to kill his father?).

Little David's failed patricide inaugurates my final two weeks chairing my college's Creative Writing Department: I started the job back on 8/10/15, a few days after a supercell thunderstorm slammed a gigantic hundred-year-old oak branch into my parked car, crushing it, a harbinger not lost on me tonight, 5/15/17, watching Episode 648 with Liz and recollecting the daily anxiety of chairing, the damage done these two years toiling as a middle-management donkey for a utilitarian upper administration running an arts school like it was Procter & Gamble—if only I could recover as quickly as Joe Haskell, who just returned from a 21-episode absence (barely a month in daily soap opera time) inexplicably cured of vampirism, sauntering into the Great House foyer, hands in his trench coat pockets, flashing a sprite smile like he just summered on Cape Cod and not Collinsport Hospital with two supernatural fang wounds on his neck; "I'm fine, right back to normal," he says to Mrs. Stoddard, who seems cured of the witch Cassandra's spell that drove her into a fugue the final months of 1968, tormenting the Collins family matriarch with visions of her own premature burial—

"Chairing the department stole two years from my life, it broke me like a wild horse," I said to Liz, which seemed hyperbolic as soon as the words came out because the truth was quite the opposite: supervising 75 full- and part-time faculty, 300 students, and a three-million-dollar budget (minus the half million the school forced me to cut during my term) cured my irrational belief I was somehow an impostor in academia—the boy who grew up with his family's meals partially subsidized by welfare and his father's nonunion factory job always on the precipice of a layoff, the boy whose hyperlexia got him promoted to third grade in the middle of second but who hunched his shoulders every night to protect himself from a vampire as his parents groomed him to be the first to attend college (the more I read and learned, the more I became estranged from my family, which no one anticipated because nobody else had gone away to college), the "rustic working-class boy from *Deer Hunter* country," as I sarcastically described myself to friends in graduate school (my self-mocking ironic pose, a flimsy defense mechanism when I felt snubbed by academia's invisible, rigid class hierarchies)—I was actually *not* a charlatan whose masquerade could be exposed at any moment, and I've now come to believe the demolished car that marked the beginning of my two years steering one of the country's largest Creative Writing departments through end-times financial austerity—shock capitalism at its worst (*What programs will I have to cut? How many classes will I be forced to add to the faculty teaching load to reduce our budget deficit? Oh, universe, prove to me you're not indifferent, don't make me have to fire anyone*)—was a different kind of portent than I originally presumed: what was broken got repaired after all (my insurance agent found a genius auto body shop), and when my chair contract ends two weeks from now, I'll begin reconstructing what it crushed in me, assuming the rule of law doesn't collapse over the summer—a phrase that comes to mind instantaneously in the Trump era when I speak in the future tense; where my parents appended the phrase "God willing" to this kind of talk, I substitute "assuming the rule of law doesn't collapse," a realistic fear less than a half year into the Trump presidency, the future of the country even gloomier since last week, when Trump fired the director of the FBI for refusing to drop the investigation into his possible collusion with Russia during the election, which, if true, would be grounds for charging the president of the United States with treason—Trump's second Nixon-like Saturday Night Massacre in the past four months (the first, in January, when he terminated the acting attorney general), firing high-level subordinates for pledging loyalty to the law, not to him.

Late-May bloom among the totalitarian: tufts of pollen piling on the street and the spicy smell of lilacs wafting through our windows recall the day everything turned last year, 6/7/16, when I received a prolonged ovation from my administrative colleagues on the Dean's Council for eliminating $33,000 from the Creative Writing budget ("I want to smell the breeze and not think of cutting budgets," I texted Liz that morning); the applause for my (coerced) evisceration of our department was inappropriately lusty and rousing, as loud as any I'd previously received for a poetry reading or musical performance, and this memory of a clapping Dean's Council shakes my nearly-done-with-chairing equilibrium today, 5/23/17, forcing me to rewind three times before I can fully focus my attention on clairvoyant Madame Findley, whom Mrs. Stoddard hired to investigate why David and Amy have been acting strangely since Collinwood's most recent séance (would've been cheaper just to consult *The Turn of the Screw*) and whose psychic ability is thrown into panic by undead perturbations in Quentin's room inside the walls of the Great House—the empty wooden ghost cradle rocks and the nineteenth-century telephone with severed wires won't stop ringing, forcing Findley to wedge herself awkwardly around the giant, wine-dark Victrola horn (baroque white roses painted inside) every time she walks to the other side of the room to answer it, the phonograph playing "Quentin's Theme" on spectral repeat; revisiting my desperate text to Liz from last June's five-hour Dean's Council budget meeting, I'm struck by how the job itself became, against my will, an essential spiritual practice, a continuous reenactment, like a recurring dream, of my favorite and most challenging passage in the *Dhammapada*: "If, like a broken bell, / You do not reverberate, / Then you have attained Nirvana / And no hostility is found in you"—

which brings back Matthew Burgess's prophetic words after his 2015 poetry reading in Chicago, around the time I was named chair: "The job will be your guru," he said, although he forgot to add that, as spiritual masters go, this one would be a sadist. My vicious guru orchestrated day-to-day bureaucratic catastrophes in which the sky fell down and I stitched it back together so it could collapse again tomorrow—an office culture of perpetual crisis and adrenaline rush that produced weekly panic attacks and epic insomnia like nothing I'd experienced since the time, 12 years ago, when personal battles with a colleague veered so far off the rails that one night I drank an entire bottle of Chianti just to go to sleep—but the wretched business of chairing finally ended today, 6/1/17, the first morning in two years I've awakened without a couple screens' worth of new emails to answer, the first time in two years I haven't worried about enrollment decreases or budget shortfalls, a day Barnabas proposes to Vicki (too soon: she's still pining for her husband to return from the eighteenth century, where Barnabas was born, bitten, died, buried, then rose again in fulfillment of a witch's curse) and Liz and I buy Dracula plants (scientific name, *Celosia cristata*; requiring full sunlight, ironically, or they will die) for our back porch after I watch *Dark Shadows* as *Not-the-Chair* for the first time in 82 episodes.

Joan Bennett (Mrs. Stoddard) has collapsed—too bad director Lela Swift neglected to inform the camera operator, positioned among the three caskets inside the Collins family tomb, that she'd actually faint *outside*, after shuffling through Eagle Hill Cemetery's shaggy grass and gravestones in her black mourning gown, muttering once again about being buried alive (evidently, she *hasn't* been cured of the witch Cassandra's curse); it's the first time in months she actually had the opportunity to act—to perform rather than just deliver morose recitations—but, poor Joan, the scene wasn't blocked properly, which makes her fall almost impossible to see without a frame-by-frame examination, my face pressed a couple inches from the computer monitor to study the baffling shot more closely: half-hidden from the camera by Little Orphan Amy standing in the mausoleum doorway, Joan's murky silhouette teeters, buckles at the waist, and then gently crumples to the ground—a curtsy of a collapse—all but ignored by a camera preoccupied with Amy's bizarre ensemble of kelly green overcoat, dark green shiny velvet dress, and bow flats the color of green M&Ms. How far we've all fallen since then: five hours after Barnabas and Mrs. Stoddard flub six lines in one scene (we love you Joan get up) and Amy confesses she's afraid of the moon but doesn't know why, the crew of Apollo 8 broadcasts a Christmas Eve 1968 message on prime-time television, astronaut Jim Lovell describing the otherworldly lunar vision outside their spaceship window, "The vast loneliness up here of the moon is awe-inspiring, and it makes you realize just what you have back there on Earth," and 49 years after Lovell and his crew become the first human beings to orbit the moon, the president of the United States tweets a video of himself wrestling and punching a man whose head has been replaced with a CNN logo, prompting journalist Jared Yates Sexton to tweet: "And for those who think there's nothing behind Trump's CNN gif today, I've been told twice in [the] past hour I'll be killed in a new Civil War." Werewolf Chris Jennings falls backward onto his bed, stabbed in the shoulder by Joe Haskell during another night of furry, full-moon marauding—Chris's hunched, lycanthropic silhouette prowled outside Joe's window before he smashed it, as Barnabas did, striking my street-facing bedroom window with his wolf's-head cane in a recurring dream— but instead of the usual brooding over my childhood nightmares, I've found myself preoccupied all day by an anonymous Reddit user's response to Sexton, "If I could slit his flabby neck and dump him in a ditch somewhere without getting caught, I absolutely would in a heartbeat," and later, I'll wake up with middle-of-the-night insomnia fixated on another anonymous response to Sexton I read online today: "When will the civil war finally happen in the U.S.? Remember, physical removal is the only solution—time for discussion is over." No surprise that Ginsberg's *The Fall of America* has been on my mind lately, a book that felt like agitprop melodrama for so many years but now, with each day unfolding like the prelude to a new civil war, I understand his "Poems of These States" better than ever before—it's not a metaphor, Ginsberg felt he was witnessing the literal fall of America and he worried the damage would take generations to rebuild (assuming, of course, the rule of law didn't collapse entirely); if psychopaths on discussion boards in 2017 are emboldened by the White House to "slit [the] flabby neck" of any journalist they disagree with, then we're closer to civil breakdown than any time in the last half century: we can't levitate Mar-a-Lago or exorcise the White House—we're stuck right now, like Chris Jennings, who takes three of Dr. Hoffman's sedatives assuming they'll knock him out long enough to sleep through the full moon but finds himself wide awake in the middle of the night, covered in fur, snarling through the accumulating drool of his fangy underbite.

Independence Day Haiku, 2017

Little David prank
calls the funeral parlor—
a ghost told him to.

The scent of Vicki's lilac perfume
creeps into the Great House from

the eighteenth century, and her clothes,
stored in the basement, have mysteriously

appeared inside her bedroom armoire—
Collinwood more hexed than usual tonight,

7/20/17, as I celebrate my mother's
birthday (she would've been 91)

with a return to the belovèd couplet,
a sentence for the episode we watched

together New Year's Eve afternoon, 1968,
when Collinwood's haunted children,

David and Amy, possessed by the ghost
of Quentin Collins, creepy-crawled

the Great House, secretly moving
Vicki's clothes from their basement

packing boxes and hanging them
in her armoire—just 11 episodes

after trying to murder David's father,
Roger—shades of the Manson Family's

middle-of-the-night excursions
they called "creepy-crawls,"

clandestine missions in which they snuck
into random homes and rearranged

the furniture while the occupants slept;
later that same night, after the credits

rolled and the calendar was turning
to 1969, Charles Manson unveiled

"Helter Skelter" to his followers over
a Death Valley campfire, preaching

for the first time his batshit apocalyptic
vision of a race war they'd survive

hiding in a magic city in a bottomless pit
in the desert, waiting out Armageddon

far removed from the cities where
blacks would vanquish whites,

after which the Family would emerge
to rule the world as hippie-KKK royalty

—according to Manson, "blackie"
lacked the necessary leadership skills

to govern a post-apocalyptic planet;
on this last night of 1968, a year when

125 U.S. cities burned in response to
Martin Luther King Jr.'s assassination

—here in Chicago, a two-mile stretch
of the West Side was destroyed—

Manson delivered his fire sermon
(at his back in a cold blast he heard

the rattle of the bones, and Helter
Skelter spread from ear to ear),

which became the cult's controlling
mythos, triggering eight months

of homicidal doomsday prepping
in 1969: countless spring and summer

creepy-crawls as they amassed an
arsenal of rifles, pistols, and knives—

and retrofitted their dune buggies
with machine-gun mounts—

while they searched the desert for
a giant hole somehow bottomless

and capable of hiding an entire city.
Happy New Year, 1969, watching

Episode 658 with Liz on the 19th
anniversary of my move from Boston

to Chicago, asking each other how
director Henry Kaplan, in only his

fifth *Dark Shadows* episode since
January 1967, convinced ABC

to devote half an episode (nine
minutes and 56 seconds, timed

on my stopwatch) to a dream sequence,
Joe Haskell's nightmare of being my

toddler self, chased out of the Collins
mausoleum by a vampire and into

the furry clutches of a werewolf—
Liz and I sitting on the bed, my laptop

between us, in a cottage we rented
this week in San Diego, an emergency

trip to see my dear cousin Michael,
a brother to me, struck yesterday

by a *demand ischemia* — in lay terms,
a mild heart attack — triggered when

he passed a gallstone a few hours after
eating lobster tacos at a Vegas casino:

terrifying to see him in the hospital
attached to a machine that took his

blood pressure at exact half-hour
intervals and displayed the results

alongside the oscillating waves
of his EKG graph on a monitor

above his head, wrenching to go
home without him that first night

—nothing suggests the shock
of mortality like the first time

you leave a loved one behind to spend
the night in a hospital ("There was

a heart attack," Trish said, "and now
we're middle-aged"); later, as I took

the *Dark Shadows* disc from my external
DVD drive, I recalled Michael introducing

me to this project's earliest inspiration,
On Kawara's *Today* series: 3,000 paintings

composed in over 112 cities, each one
nothing but a monochromatic rendering

of the month, day, and year it was
created, a multi-painting experiment

in autobiography that ended only
when Kawara died: Michael and I

saw several pieces from the *Today*
series at the Chicago MCA in 1998,

a few days after I moved here,
and once he explained Kawara's

procedural strategies, his texts and
contexts, it became clear immediately

that I had to find a way to translate
the visual and conceptual thrill

of the date paintings into writing —
not knowing the right Kawara-like

poetry project wouldn't find me until
13 years later, when I composed my first

Dark Shadows sentence on 5/31/11;
our week in San Diego evoked

memories of similar trips I made
to Pennsylvania the first decade

of the 2000s for family illnesses,
hospitalizations, and deaths,

the losses I wrote about in Book 2
of this undead poem — my adored

phantoms who float at the corners
of vision every night I slip a *Dark*

Shadows disc into the DVD player
—but now, after the hospital,

with medications and dietary changes
to prevent a future *demand ischemia*,

I can say, thank you, Michael, for knowing
how deeply I'd fall for the *Today* series,

for insisting we go to the MCA
that week in '98 you visited my

ex-wife Shelly and me, right after
we moved to Chicago, your presence

soothing when I was hobbled
by worries I'd made the worst

decision of my life, leaving a city,
Boston, where I forged friendships

close enough they are family,
where I recorded and toured

with my band, Drumming on Glass
(flash of memory from 1990, wearing

a T-shirt silk-screened with the words
All art must be clearly labeled the night

we gathered to celebrate signing with
our record label, Aurora), and where,

in 1997, I helped create an alternative
economic system for our neighborhood,

the Fenway Skills Exchange, in which
neighbors paid each other for services

like tutoring, babysitting, shopping,
apartment cleaning, website design,

and dog walking, among others,
in "Fenway Tenders," a paper currency

I printed on my desktop computer,
each Fenway Tender worth an hour

of our neighbor's time; what a crushing
fall from grace, moving out of the Fenway

in 1998 for my first full-time teaching
job, at Harper College in Palatine,

a Chicago suburb a few miles north
of the local Ikea, where aluminum siding

seems to grow right out of the ground
(our college president threatened to shoot

the ducks that swam the campus pond—
his demented vision of thinning the herd

—when he wasn't telling stories at faculty
meetings about reading *The Wall Street*

Journal to his wife every morning
in his boxer shorts), my worst Chicago

fears confirmed when we moved
into our first neighborhood, Bucktown:

an artists' haven in the early '90s,
the area was, by 1998, a gentrified

enclave of isolated families, thirty-
somethings living in million-dollar

McMansions who pushed us off
the sidewalk when they passed by

in their double-wide baby strollers.
Despite the confident tone of my

previous sentence, tracing this poem's
archaeological roots, I've actually

spent the month of July worried I'm
tethered to a project I won't be able

to finish, anxious I'll exhaust myself
or die before I can write this poem's

1,225th sentence; I'm so far from
shore in Book 3 that I can't see where

the poem started or where it might
end, but today, on the western edge

of the country, on vacation with Liz
in Mendocino, California—drinking

coffee every morning on our balcony
after meditation, then breakfast and

a walk to see horses, donkeys, and llamas
eat grass and meander the vegan resort

where we're staying (my reward
for surviving two besieged years

in academic middle management
as the department chair donkey)—

today, watching *Dark Shadows* after
another morning with the animals,

Little David, the psychic child,
developed a photo of Carolyn

and Barnabas in his personal Great
House darkroom and a ghost-

image of Vicki hanging by the neck
in 1796 (convicted of witchcraft)

inexplicably appeared—hovering above
Carolyn and Barnabas, the eighteenth

century imposing itself once again
on the twentieth—which helped me

understand the past month's *Dark
Shadows* anxiety a little better:

I've been panicking in clock-time
about a poem that takes place

out of time, fretting that readers
might grow bored with the calendar's

slow turn, episode by episode,
each new sentence nesting deeper

into an asynchronous tangle of soap
opera time travel and personal memory,

but the shock of the psychic child's
unintentional spirit photography

(his ghoulish, soap-snuff image
recalling Episode 460, when

viewers saw the soundstage gallows
rope swing, choking Vicki to death)

somehow freed me from my distress
that readers will grow tired of this

poem's relentless dailiness—
monotony, after all, is actually

built into the poem's architecture
like the necessary boredom of my

daily meditation practice, softening
the mind's greed for new experiences

("Mountains never get tired of being
mountains," as Chögyam Trungpa

Rinpoche once wrote, "and waterfalls
never get tired of being waterfalls"):

O, how boring I am, the writer of
this endless poem, 777 episodes to go—

including the one I'm watching now
—I sit, breathe, watch TV, then do it

all over again for the next sentence,
a repetition that can be numbing,

but if I'm trying to shape a memoir-
poem without forcing a plot or master

narrative upon it, then I have to admit
some of the most intimate, vulnerable

moments of our lives are those
that seem mundane when we

live them: drinking morning coffee,
watching the fog crawl back over

Mendocino Bay, talking to a sweet
donkey who saunters from his food

trough to greet me and stares back
with soft, bulbous black eyes while

I singsong-jabber at him like I'm
chatting with a two-year-old —

or, later tonight, sitting on the bed,
scrolling through Facebook to pass

the boring time and finding a review
by Alex Gildzen of Book 2 of this poem,

Inside the Walls of My Own House,
that reminds me each sentence

I write accumulates, slowly,
unencumbered by calendar-time,

into living theater: "I saw Jonathan
Frid [Barnabas Collins] perform

Shakespeare 2 years & 3 months
before Tony Trigilio was born,"

Alex writes, "I saw Joan Bennett
[Mrs. Stoddard] perform Kaufman

& Hart 2 years & one month after
he was born. This masterwork

makes me think my own autobio
while enjoying Tony's, but of course

it's so much more than his
life: it's also an epic long poem,

it intertwines the life of a person
with the life of a soap opera while

revealing what poetry is & how it's
made. The levels of this ongoing

project seem endless. This is
the first nite in my new residence

that I've snuggled up with a book.
It feels good. I'm on the verge

of a cheap vampire reference
so I'll stop with the hope Tony

& I enjoy long lives. I want
him to complete his poem

& I want to be able to read it."

The great estate of Collinwood on a solemn evening. On this night, an incident in the long-dead past has intruded on the present.

The night holds many terrors for those who live at Collinwood.

The secrets of time and space are no longer a mystery to one man at Collinwood.

Night at Collinwood, but this is not Collinwood as it exists in the present.

Northeast Ohio Terza Rima

I watched four episodes in Cleveland
(A Rust Belt reading tour for Book 2),
Hoarding the introductory teasers

In my notebook, remixing them into
A "Night at Collinwood" half-page collage
Of found text, my reward for sitting through

An entire clip show with laptop wedged
Between my knees in my hotel while
Episode 661 flashed back (footage dredged

From ABC's *Dark Shadows* video archive,
The tapes damaged, of course, their colors
Washed-out and grainy) to the 1795 plotline,

Which droned interminably for a hundred
Episodes in 1967-68. And now, in the century
That bored me to death, Barnabas is hunting

Prostitutes on the wharf again, biting necks
While Victoria Winters awaits the gallows:
Tonight, in Chicago, haunted by memories

Of Victoria hanged—a death so harrowing
ABC keeps restaging it—I'll compose an extra
Sentence to mark my reading at hallowed

Mac's Backs bookstore last week (the epicenter
Of Cleveland's literary scene), not for nostalgia
But for what poetry enables: to remember

That touring in 2017 for this multivolume
Poem brought me together with friends
And fellow writers otherwise impossible

To see this year: Diana Hume George, Kenneth
Ross, Alec Niedenthal, Barb Tan, Albert Mobilo,
Hafizah Geter, Darley Stewart, Eliot Katz, Dennis

Ginty, Suzanne DeGaetano, Dave Polster,
John Madera, Alex Liebergesell, Candace
Williams, Peter Hale, Deirdre Coyle, Alice Cone,

Lauren Hilger, Charles North, Rosa Ransom,
Matthew Binder, Susie Ringel, Mary Boo
Anderson, Marie Lathers, and David Hassler.

Marooned for one last episode in 1796 (Barnabas traveled back in time to prevent Victoria's hanging, as if a vampire could persuade ABC to nix its dead-damsel fetish), I'm watching Episode 666 with Liz on Halloween, 2017, two days after a man dressed as a squirrel wandered out of our downstairs neighbor's apartment and saluted with a sloshing, half-finished bottle of beer as we descended the stairs, the two of us trying to make sense of a spontaneous murder spree by gentle giant Ben Stokes, who just beat Navy Lieutenant Nathan Forbes to death and suffocated Countess du Prés, his fingers pinching her nose, meaty left hand covering her mouth, smothering her against Barnabas's empty coffin—my god, how many caskets I'd seen by age two, a veteran of hundreds of *Dark Shadows* episodes, the coffins broadcast into our living room every week combining to form a single funerary-box archetype in my psyche: the gorgeous simplicity of the typical *Dark Shadows* casket—its clean rectangular lines, worn brass handles, the dull, faded veneer of unadorned wood— was my Platonic ideal, buried in tombs and cemetery plots (or tucked away in the Old House basement), a container for the dead that taught me the dead can't be contained.

All children in Collinsport are connoisseurs of entombment: Little Orphan Amy begs Carolyn to let her play in the graveyard before breakfast and pick flowers along the way, and earlier today, while visiting David Trinidad's Foundations in Creative Writing class at Columbia College to read from Books 1 and 2 (and a work in progress from this volume, the saga of my mother's hearing loss and my first-book galleys, a timely excerpt the week before I'm scheduled to be fitted for hearing aids), a student asked why I took such pains in the first two books to emphasize my father's rote, military dailiness—he'd turn in his grave, I said, if he knew his relentless discipline, learned as a police officer in World War II, produced a Buddhist artist instead of, say, a Catholic insurance salesman and one-weekend-a-month army reservist—and another student asked if I'd learned American Sign Language since Book 1, which reminded me that I can't truly honor my years of communicating via Post-it note with my Uncle Joe, born deaf and mute, and can't burn the karma of my family's failure to learn to sign, until I take ASL classes of my own (such a close reading of one's intimate autobiographical work, I felt exposed even though I'd willingly exposed myself)—and then, with a couple minutes left in class, one last question, "Why do you think you were a religious charlatan in a previous life?" (psychic Patricia Kennedy says this about me on page 54 of Book 1), to which I replied I couldn't answer without knowing my *previous* previous life, the one before I bilked my followers, prompting a different student who'd been quiet all class to bolt up straight and tell his best friend's reincarnation story: the friend was two, his mother driving them past a dessert shop he'd never seen before, and suddenly the boy pointed out the window and blurted, "Remember when I used to take you there for ice cream?" with no idea his uncle, who died two months before he was born, used to treat the mother to ice cream there when she was a girl.

Little Orphan Amy lies about having a nightmare so Carolyn won't punish her for visiting Little David's bedroom in the middle of the night.

I couldn't escape from noise, my mother's auditory nerves irreparably damaged, her TV raised to peak loudness, garbled and distorted, my father in the front room responding in kind, turning up his TV high enough to drown out my mother's in our tiny, one-story house, three small bedrooms and a bathroom, a thousand square feet of televised clatter reverberating every night, which forced me to jack up my stereo higher and higher just to hear myself think—daily childhood cacophonies that seem more real than ever tonight, the eve of my mother's 16th death anniversary, watching *Dark Shadows* at low volume and without headphones, for once not worried the TV will wake Liz: my first episode with a water-resistant crescent moon (color: anthracite) cupping each of my ears, I'm adjusting to this amplified world 20 years earlier than the average first-time hearing-aid user, the full frequency range of the Great House reaching my newly cybernetic ear canal for once without maximum blare as Amy and David shuffle gigantic playing cards twice the size of their hands, the psychic child plunking down a massive ace of spades, a curse on Mrs. Johnson, who just returned to Collinwood after an 11-episode absence.

Carolyn, who once tried to run away with an artificial man stitched together from dead body parts, nervously touches her flat-ironed, blonde hair as she reveals to Chris Jennings, who turns into a wolf every 30 days, that she'd planned a surprise romantic Sunday excursion with him—at which point, a maroon pentagram suddenly superimposes itself, chroma-keyed, upon her face. Cursed by love and low-budget satanic special effects, Carolyn intones today's episode introduction: it's time for her latest interspecies love interest to succumb to the full moon and "experience a painful and hideous transformation from man to predatory animal." Later, while taking her daily stroll to the mausoleum, hoping to witness her mother rise from the dead (which in Collinsport is always a fifty-fifty possibility), Carolyn is attacked by the werewolf she doesn't know is actually the man she wants to take for a lover; after the wolfman chases her back to the Great House, she encounters her dazed and freshly resurrected mother, Mrs. Stoddard, still dressed in her burgundy burial gown, leaning against the long wooden table in the foyer where the Collins family black telephone sits next to a sculpture of a shirtless worker shoveling peat in a bog.

Richard Nixon begins his first term
as president dodging a hail of rocks,
smoke bombs, and tomatoes thrown
at his motorcade—not that anyone's
paying attention in haunted Collinsport,
where Mrs. Stoddard just escaped
the grave and a full moon illuminates
the furry body of Little Orphan Amy's
brother, Chris Jennings, slumped and
growling over a boulder while the mute
nineteenth-century ghost of Beth Chavez,
stiff in her white silk, lace-collared,
Turn of the Screw gown, weeps over
the barely conscious werewolf.
      "There is one possible
explanation: a man turned into an animal,"
Barnabas says, an appropriate epitaph
for 2017, Trump's first year in office
now just 13 days from its finish,
still plenty of time for him to hasten
the end of the American experiment,
the *Washington Post* reporting today
that the White House barred
Centers for Disease Control scientists
from using the words *evidence-based*,
science-based, *vulnerable*, *diversity*,
fetus, *entitlement*, and *transgender*,
calling to mind Kim Jong Un's
proclamation last year banning sarcasm
in North Korea: I now live in a country
that forbids its scientists from saying
"evidence-based" to describe
knowledge they acquire from studying
evidence, an intractable nation,
Whitman's "fabled damned"
suddenly on a bizarre mission
to become a petty Dada kleptocracy,

our paranoid Dear Leader wolfing
down McDonald's cheeseburgers in bed
every night, certain the fast-food chain's
burgers are his only protection against
being poisoned—we've been kidnapped
by a time machine and dropped
into Ceaușescu's Romania, where
the dictator nicknamed "Draculescu"
reclines within the padded walls
and gilded draperies of the private
cinema in his Spring Palace basement
watching *Kojak* reruns in his bathrobe
while his country trades strawberries
for fighter planes.
                Paying attention
is an act of survival, until it creeps
over the line into obsession and
I catch myself constantly left-swiping
my phone every hour for the latest
updates from Draculescu's crypt:
reading Twitter's "Trending News"
ticker is like drinking from Sheriff
Patterson's unwashed watercooler—
it's convenient and seems effortless
until you realize (too late) you've
forced the body to overheat
digesting the filth you just swallowed
(tonight, the Sheriff's final *Dark Shadows*
appearance, and Vince O'Brien,
the fourth actor to play Patterson
since the character's debut 621 episodes
ago, marks the occasion by offering
a glass of dirty water to console
a werewolf victim's grieving friend)—
and though I agree with Auden,
"There is no such thing as the State,"
I'm compelled to study each new tweet

from the crypt, like today's penis-fight
Armageddon proxy—
> "North Korean leader Kim Jong Un
> just stated that the 'Nuclear Button
> is on his desk at all times,'" Trump wrote,
> adding, "Will someone from his
> depleted and food starved regime
> please inform him that I too have
> a Nuclear Button, but it is a much
> bigger & more powerful one
> than his, and my Button works!"

—for signs we'll have to flee the country:
my father fought Nazis, which made
history real for me at a very young age,
and one of my earliest memories
(predating even my *Dark Shadows*
nightmares) is a vision I experienced
while he changed my diaper one night,
of black-clad, swastika'd soldiers
goose-stepping down our street,
a ghostly dreamlike scene that,
to this day, feels like a memory of a real
Nazi memory, a past-life regression
that insinuated its way into the present
—reminding me of Philip K. Dick's
famous 1974 vision, while recovering
from dental surgery, of ancient Rome
superimposed on his quiet
Berkeley neighborhood,
a phantasm that transformed his
conception of reality ("I hadn't gone
back in time," he wrote to a friend
later that year, "but in a sense Rome
had come forward, by insidious and sly
degrees, under new names, hidden by
the flak talk and phony obscurations,
at last into our world again")—

                    my father explained
many times over the years that the war
was the singular defining experience
of his life, which made total sense to me,
as a child, because Hitler chose to invade
Poland on my father's 18th birthday,
and I listened closely to his stories,
the least I could do to show respect for
what he (excitedly) endured in wartime
England and France, where he earned
the nickname "Frenchy" for the bits
of language he picked up as a soldier
—and the great fear his war instilled
was that somehow I'd make the same
mistake as those who stayed
too long in Europe between the wars,
ordinary people who trusted the civil
mechanisms of the State so much
they were content to wait until the next
election, when, surely, the Nazis
would be voted out of power.

Visiting Liz's parents in their Sarasota condo, reading
the latest news updates in the shade of sheltering
palms: Chicago trapped in a late-December ice storm
while my childhood city, Erie, Pennsylvania, digs out
from a record 53-inch snowfall the morning after David
and Amy stage a *Village of the Damned* staredown with
Mrs. Johnson—"We're not staring at you," David says
in homicidal deadpan, "we're just watching you
work"—while playing War with the mammoth deck of
cards introduced seven episodes ago (twice the size of
their hands), followed by yet another secret meeting
between the psychic child and the ghost of Quentin
Collins in the abandoned West Wing of the Great
House, where the mutton-chopped specter (mute, as
always, in his frock coat) telepathically guides Little
David to a bottle of strychnine hidden in the West
Wing's nineteenth-century rolltop desk.

Dr. Hoffman's *Bride of Frankenstein* artificial woman died on the operating table, and she failed to cure Barnabas's vampirism with plasma injections—but there's no reason to believe she won't solve Chris Jennings's werewolf curse by reading *The Lycanthrope of Angers* (rhymes with "toupee"), the true story of Jacques Roulet, a sixteenth-century beggar tried for murder, lycanthropy, and cannibalism who testified in court that his parents bestowed upon him a magic ointment that shape-shifted his body into a werewolf's every full moon (Roulet found guilty and sentenced to death, which on appeal to the Parlement of Paris, was commuted to "two years imprisonment in a madhouse, that he might be instructed in the knowledge of God, whom he had forgotten in his utter poverty"). Wearing a chalky, mint-pink, powdered sugar nightgown—a Necco Wafer monstrosity—Hoffman shuffles around the Great House with a remarkable lack of urgency for a doctor awaiting an emergency shipment of atropine to save a wolfman from strychnine poisoning. Denise Nickerson (Little Orphan Amy) badgers the truth out of David— the strychnine came from Quentin's ghost—with the same high-pitched hectoring that she'd perfect two years later, as the gum-chewing blueberry brat Violet Beauregarde in *Willy Wonka & the Chocolate Factory*, which the children in Jonestown watched on the last morning of their lives—imported American videotapes one of the few luxuries afforded them in the isolated Guyanese rain forest—not knowing of course that Gene Wilder's sadistic chocolatier was unwittingly preparing them for the brutality to come hours later that day, November 18, 1978, in the utopian settlement's main pavilion, when the adults squirted syringes of cyanide-laced grape Flavor Aid into their mouths.

Little David steps from a hiding
spot next to his dresser and launches
a disoriented soliloquy, a catatonic
recitation of seventeenth-century
poet Tom Brown's nursery rhyme,
"I do not like thee, Doctor Fell"
("The reason why, I cannot tell,"
the psychic child drones, his effort
to stare portentously at the camera
coming off as groggy improvisation),
and as the camera inches closer
to his mouth, I cannot help but wince
remembering tonight's opening scene,
when the show's creator, Dan Curtis,
directing only his 13th *Dark Shadows*
episode, steered the camera into
Little David's face, subjecting
the psychic child to a close-up
so tight it revealed a constellation
of five zits along his right nostril
and cheek—poor David Henesy,
his adolescence unfolding in harshly lit,
saturated Technicolor every weekday
from 4:00-4:30—and no matter how
hard Curtis tries to redirect our attention
to other objects in his bedroom,
I cannot take my mind off David's
pimpled face, even as the camera
lingers an extra beat on a paper doll
standing on the dresser behind
the psychic child, an orange-faced
little girl with long, fuchsia hair and
rosy cheeks, holding a protest sign
that reads, CHICKEN LITTLE WAS RIGHT—
        the episode bumping along
like a precarious schooner in Curtis's
hands ever since Joan Bennett's
(Mrs. Stoddard's) exquisite flub

at the 4:18 mark: a quick gasp of air
in midsentence of a lifeless speech
about Little David's table manners,
after which she licked her lips
(nervous tic) and instantly gave up
on the lines she'd forgotten, the sky
falling on the Collins family matriarch,
prompting me to capture the scene
on my phone and send it to David
Trinidad, who texted back a couple
hours later:
        "I love this—god, Joan is brilliant—
she needed to wet her whistle,"
his reply arriving as I sat down
to read *Barnabas Collins in a Funny
Vein*, a 1969 mass-market paperback
collection of Barnabas jokes
David bought at an antique mall
in the "Quilt Capital of Iowa,"
Kalona, an Amish town located
twenty miles southwest of Iowa City
—a book I probably wouldn't have
understood as a child watching *Dark
Shadows* every day with my mother,
too young to know the difference
between terror and camp—
my favorite gag, "When you sleep
in Barnabas's guest room,
you don't sleep on a bed of roses,
you sleep on a bed of neurosis,"
isn't really a joke at all, but instead
a straightforward depiction
of my childhood insomnia,
hunching my shoulders every night
in bed to protect myself against
the two-centuries-old vampire;
"I expect to see some of those jokes
mentioned in the poem," David said

a few days later, hanging out
in my office before our Tuesday
afternoon classes, "it's not often
I give you a gift with strings attached"
                        —but actually
this is the third time in the last six
years I've received a gift from him
with *Dark Shadows* strings: in 2012,
for my 46th birthday, he bought me
Dario Argento's 1977 horror
masterpiece, *Suspiria*, starring Joan
Bennett, adding a note I later quoted
on pages 51-52 of the first volume
of this poem, "I expect to see this
mentioned in *Dark Shadows*," he wrote,
"don't you love a present with
strings attached!", a theme David
repeated in 2014, when he gave me
a replica of Barnabas's infamous
black onyx ring, accompanied by
a birthday greeting he composed
on the back of a movie postcard
for Hitchcock's *Vertigo*, where he
summoned Kobayashi Issa's famous
dewdrop-world haiku to summon
himself back into this poem:

        "For Tony—another
        present with no strings.
        And yet . . . . And yet . . . ."

Returning to the show after nearly a month-long absence (still queasy, fixated on the bulbous pimple hugging the bottom of Little David's right nostril), I'm watching *Dark Shadows* in Tampa, psychologically barricaded in my hotel room, dreading a looming three-day schmooze with 10,000 other writers at the AWP Conference (introvert hell), the midday Florida sun glancing off my laptop screen as Little David once again slips into "Doctor Fell" nonsense; later, after a mute consultation with the frock-coated ghost of Quentin Collins, the psychic child breaks into a song (to the tune of "Yankee Doodle Dandy") about "Mr. Juggins," a mannequin with mutton chops Magic-Markered on his face whose mere presence gaslights Maggie into retracting her claim she saw a real ghost amid the cobwebbed junk pile of the abandoned West Wing (according to *The Dark Shadows Almanac*, the song was an inside joke among the cast, an homage to the show's boom-mic operator, Max Jughans, who notoriously couldn't keep the microphone from dropping into camera view).

Maggie consults with Mrs. Johnson about ghosts they've both seen—an urgency in their voices, an unspoken understanding that they know the difference between supernatural mutton chops and those drawn with black Magic Marker—and Professor Stokes concludes that Collinwood needs another séance (of course), this time to summon Janet Findley, the psychic who collapsed from a heart attack and fell down the grand staircase of the Great House 33 episodes ago, frightened to death by the spirits she had been hired to contact.

Barnabas exhumes an unknown child's coffin with Chris Jennings but I have to squint to make out the details, everything fuzzy and blurred—a damaged, black-and-white kinescope copy is all that remains of Episode 683—the close-ups resembling charcoal portraits, especially in this final scene, Barnabas's bear-claw comb-over smudged across his forehead as he and Chris inspect the mysterious casket they just unearthed among the grayscaled tombstones of Eagle Hill Cemetery. "It certainly isn't the *pine box* of the earlier period," Barnabas says to Chris, admiring the tiny coffin, adding to the morbid catalogue of tombs and caskets broadcast into my home every afternoon as a boy, this one the final resting place of an infant buried with a pentagram medallion clasped around its neck, a werewolf talisman made by doomed Collinsport jeweler Ezra Braithwaite, played by Abe Vigoda, who in three years will betray Michael Corleone in *The Godfather*, and then three years later will complain about his hemorrhoids in *Barney Miller*, but who in 1969 sits beneath a gaggle of cuckoo clocks in his centuries-old family silver shop and clownishly barks at customers over the telephone in a grouchy Maine brogue.

Mrs. Stoddard pulls on her dyed candy-apple red, camel-hair overcoat and opens the grand double doors of the Great House—it was evening all afternoon in Collinwood, it was thundering and it was going to thunder without rain the rest of the episode.

I can't resist a bonus sentence after camera operator
Stuart Goodman's DVD extra interview reveals that you
didn't have to be stalked by a 208-year-old vampire to
be frightened every weekday afternoon after *One Life to
Live*: "We'd do it like it was live," Goodman said of the
relentless daily shooting schedule and sets so small the
cameras often bumped into each other, "and some days,
when the tape machine wasn't working, we actually
went on live, which was really scary for not only us but
the other actors."

Told that Abe Vigoda's cranky silversmith, Ezra Braithwaite, was pronounced dead of "heart failure" (instead of, more accurately, "choked to death by nineteenth-century ghost"), Barnabas raises a skeptical voice above the din of another episode-long, dry thunderstorm: "The same explanation for *Janet Findley's* death, too," he says, adding, "Curious, *so many* hearts should stop in this house," a moment of rare vocal command for someone who usually can't deliver his lines without bumbling, but he's quickly back in character and tripping over the script in the very next scene: "Braithwaite knew who he had sold that book to—that, that *pentagram*—so many years ago" (yes, Robert Hass, "a word is elegy to what it signifies," except on *Dark Shadows*, where a word—*any* word—is elegy for what cannot be memorized).

~

Dr. Hoffman reprises the ending of yesterday's episode—a husky gasp, the inane flutter of her gigantic false eyelashes—stumbling upon Beth Chavez's photograph in a nineteenth-century Collins family album in the abandoned West Wing of the Great House and exclaiming in her croaky smoker's rasp, "It's the *same* woman who led us to Chris Jennings's cottage," as if the *Turn of the Screw* evening gown Beth wore the night she guided Hoffman and Barnabas to the cottage somehow wasn't a dead giveaway that Chavez was a ghost from another century—then again, who am I to judge Hoffman's fright, experiencing my own today, privately, alone in our apartment and watching *Dark Shadows* on the 48th anniversary of the Kent State murders, distraught that we've swiftly normalized the day-to-day cruelty of the past year and a half, ruled by a president who consorts with dictators and actually threatens to jail his political opponents—how quaint that we were shocked in 1970 when the military fired on its own people in Kent—but there's no time to brood, the West Wing door just mysteriously slammed shut and gusts from the spirit world blew back the ancient room's dirty, pink curtains and snuffed out the candles, prompting another exaggerated reaction shot from Hoffman, who flips the back of her hand against her open mouth like a silent film star, a contorted burst of movement that, on this awful remembrance day, recalls for me the abject fear I felt last year—typical of the silent-movie hyperbole of my own imagination—when I sat through "Workplace Active Shooter Training" and faculty were told our first response in a mass shooting should be to "Run: escape, call 911," and if we can't, then we should "Hide: out of shooter's view, barricade doors, silence phones," and if all else fails, "Fight: as a last resort and only when your life is in imminent danger."

Sylvia Plath sees Joan Bennett perform in *Bell, Book and Candle* on 1/20/53 at the Court Square Theater in Springfield, Massachusetts (thirteen years before Bennett begins her role as Elizabeth Stoddard, the haunted, sherry-swilling matriarch of the Collins family), and the following day in a letter to her mother Plath describes the play as "a heavenly humorous tale of modern witchery," a witchy tidbit I owe to David Trinidad, who discovered it in *The Letters of Sylvia Plath, Volume 1: 1940-1956* (a 1,424-page archival trove edited by Peter K. Steinberg and Karen V. Kukil), emailing the information to me the morning I witnessed the return of gargly-voiced actor Roger Davis, who, as Peter Bradford, fell for Victoria Winters during her eighteenth-century witchcraft trial and then, as moony-eyed Jeff Clark, married Victoria in the twentieth century, and who today—take a deep breath, we're off and running with yet another soap opera doppelgänger charade—rapped on the grand double doors of the Great House in his first appearance as Ned Stuart, an old friend of werewolf Chris Jennings (played by Don Briscoe, who also performed the role of Chris's identical twin brother, handyman-turned-vampire Tom Jennings), a whiplash plot swerve in the middle of a loony mash-up of *The Wolf Man* and *The Turn of the Screw* that has slowly (or, better yet, "interminably," since this particular narrative arc seems endless, playing out for 62 episodes now and counting) taken its toll on Little David, who complains to Quentin that he's constantly being tormented by the ghost of Ezra Braithwaite, whom Quentin, a ghost himself of course—more doubling! I can't keep up with it all—murdered three episodes ago; the poor psychic child, panicked and sleepless by the end of the episode, reveals to Maggie that he's turned to writing to soothe his agitated psyche, a strategy that can only end badly: "You're very pretty, Maggie," he says, shortly before the credits roll, confessing that he writes fiction when he can't get to sleep at night, "maybe someday I'll write a story about you" (oh, god, keep the little stalker away from MFA students when he grows up).

Surrounded by a swarming Fenway neighborhood lunch crowd, I sat on a bench in front of the new Target on Boylston Street in Boston, facing away from its deceptively jolly red-and-white signage as I waited for my old friend Mitch, living his third year since being diagnosed with early-onset Alzheimer's, who just texted to let me know he was stuck in traffic with his neighbor Jay, the huge *Dark Shadows* fan who showed me his DVD coffin earlier in this book (on page 41) when I visited in 2016, the two of them driving from nearby Somerville to meet me for this afternoon's Red Sox game: I stared at the six-story, luxury residential mid-rise across the street, kitty-corner from me, where the low-slung, decrepit Mass Tire building once stood and where my old band, Drumming on Glass, rehearsed in the late 1980s and early 1990s, fixing my gaze on the new building like it was some kind of divination tool (which, I realize, is an apt description of how I watch *Dark Shadows*), the passing parade of Bostonians oblivious, of course, to my descent into another New England memory fugue: a woman in a black-and-white polka-dot dress, jean jacket draped over her shoulders, sat on the bench next to me stressing over her day planner while a bearded, sunburned man in a Houston Astros baseball cap, sitting adjacent to her, wolfed down fried rice from a Styrofoam take-out box as a young couple walked by, clutching their backpack straps a little too seriously, like they were looking for a hiking trail they'd lost—at which point the armpit stench of fried, vending-cart sausages and hot dogs wafting around the corner from the Jersey Street ballpark entrance triggered a memory of a night in 1991, when I shared our rehearsal building's unisex bathroom for a few minutes with Aimee Mann (on the verge of the solo career that would resurrect her fame after 'Til Tuesday) as our bands took bathroom breaks, Mann using the stall while I peed in the urinal, overfed horseflies buzzing my face as I tried to hold my breath, determined not to inhale—the bathroom often smelled thuddingly fecal, but this night its complicated mélange of stink overwhelmed me, evoking the neglected state park restrooms of my childhood—standing a few feet from the musician whose band won the 1985 MTV Best New Artist Award for its massive hit single "Voices Carry" and releasing my stream into a urinal in a pest-stricken edifice that also was a joyous hive of art-making, where famed indie producer and recording engineer Lou Giordano, visiting our rehearsal room in 1990 during pre-production for our first album, *Asparagus Tea*, sat as far as he could from the air-conditioning vent and joked (but not really) that he was afraid he might contract Legionnaires' disease just from breathing the air in the crumbling warehouse, and as I sat in front of the new Target, waiting for Mitch and Jay, I could barely comprehend that the Soviet-style, concrete, rectilinear structure where we wrote a couple albums' worth of songs a quarter century ago had been transformed into a lavish apartment building, a black steel and glass behemoth that reeks of Mammon—just then, a phone call from Mitch broke my memory-palace reverie, an update on their traffic jam, Jay's car stuck and immobile somewhere nearby, or so it seemed, the tragicomedy of errors that is Alzheimer's preventing either of us from fully understanding each other (maybe Mitch was saying they had just parked, I couldn't really tell), and to make things worse, Mitch's phone lost reception before he could explain where they were; later, after the game, alone in my Brookline hotel watching Little Orphan Amy search for a missing jigsaw puzzle piece as she sang "Inchworm" (originally performed by Danny Kaye in the 1952 film *Hans Christian Andersen*), I offered a prayer of gratitude that Mitch, so easy to love, is surrounded by loved ones—none more caring than his wife Paula, who grew up near the Cliff Walk in Newport, Rhode Island, where the *Dark Shadows* opening title sequence, Atlantic Ocean waves crashing against a rocky shoreline, was filmed—who guide him through the treacherous, dark forest of a disease where the direct path is always lost, Alzheimer's causing random midsentence blackouts in Mitch, a fiction writer whose characters speak, as he once did but no longer can, in long, many-tentacled paragraphs: "It's a lazy executioner," Mitch said, flatly, after the game, in his Somerville living room, the two of us drinking green tea as he speculated whether he would make it to the far end of his Alzheimer's life expectancy, 20 years, and if he—or anyone—would want to live that long with the disease.

Mrs. Johnson returns after a nine-episode absence to narrate tonight's morose, droning introductory teaser: "In the Great House at Collinwood, a young woman will soon face the most terrifying experience she will ever know," she says of Maggie Evans, who opens the episode in the grip of Quentin Collins—the mutton-chopped ghost strangling her with a purple curtain sash, a spectral homicide interrupted when Mrs. J. herself stumbles upon the scene, stiff and angular in a panic-black dress topped with a prim, white lace collar, hair pulled back so severely it draws her mouth into a wince ("She looks like Emily Dickinson," Liz says, ensuring I'll no longer be able to see the Collins family maid without thinking of the famous 1848 Dickinson daguerreotype, which only makes tonight's installment of the show's ongoing Henry James/Lon Chaney Jr. mash-up even more precarious)—

forgive me, Mrs. J., as horrific as this failed ghost strangulation is for Maggie, I'm not convinced it's "the most terrifying experience she will ever know": back in '67 she was kidnapped by a 207-year-old vampire who locked her in his basement dungeon until she agreed to become his undead bride, and a year later Dr. Hoffman strapped her to an operating table in a harebrained scheme to transfer Maggie's "life force" into an artificial woman built from dead body parts (a Bride of Frankenstein who somehow resembled Helen Gurley Brown), Hoffman rolling up her sleeves and getting down to business in a shrieking mad-scientist laboratory of submarine pings, slushy feedback loops, strobe lights, and pulsing pink tuning forks—

though I admit, Mrs. J., a case can be made, all the same, that Maggie's near strangulation has triggered an unholy terror in the Great House, even if it's not "the most terrifying experience [Maggie] will ever know": Little David and Little Orphan Amy are playing nineteenth-century dress-up, spellbound by

Quentin in their *Turn of the Screw* frippery, the psychic
child flailing about in a double-breasted frock coat and
floppy bow tie, Amy following close behind in a neck-
high, floor-length lace gown, the two of them warbling
like wounded street cats as they shuffle in predatory,
asymmetrical loops around Mrs. Stoddard, frozen to
her spot and hearing for the first time the schmaltzy
strings of "Quentin's Theme" emanating from the
abandoned West Wing's wine-dark Victrola horn,
filling the Great House with a waltz that next month, in
March '69, will be nominated for a Best Instrumental
Theme Grammy, the Collins family matriarch's
cardinal-red dress perfectly matched to her lipstick
(smeared slightly, though, around her bottom lip), her
brooch polished so bright it seems to blink under the
stage lights—

        two children, possessed by
a nineteenth-century ghost, making deranged
circumambulations around a '40s film noir femme
fatale (also seen by Sylvia Plath on a witchy, western
Massachusetts stage in '53) who's probably unaware of
the lipstick streak below her bottom lip, a scene I've
rewound and watched four times just to appreciate the
diligence it took to create pandemonium on a
production schedule so tight the actors had little time to
learn their lines and block their scenes: Little David
hasn't seemed this dangerous since the night 343
episodes ago when he snuck into Carolyn Collins's
bedroom and perched himself at the foot of her bed to
watch her sleep: "I just wanted to make sure you
weren't dead," the psychic child said to Carolyn when
she woke, screaming (on page 78 of Book 1 of this
poem), recalling for me the horrifying story of Ted
Bundy, age three, creepy-crawling into his aunt's
bedroom as she slept and arranging all the kitchen
knives in a circle around her on the bed —

                so, yes, I'll give you this much,
Mrs. J., tonight's episode might not be the most

terrifying experience of *Maggie's* life, but it's the first time as an adult that I've been rattled by *Dark Shadows*—I just rewound a fifth time to watch Amy reach the precipice of a Linda Blair death-stare before Quentin literally strikes her blind—and like the stagehand who ducks out of camera view at the beginning of this maniacal scene, I'll scram from the page and give the psychic child the final word: "It's too late—it's too late to be afraid," he says in sociopathic, goth deadpan, his hair tousled in a savage coif, the little stalker breaking into a gawky cackle right before the credits roll ("This is creepier than Barnabas," Liz blurts out—easy for her to say, since, unlike me, she didn't see this episode for the first time at the age of two, shoulders hunched to protect against a vampire each night before going to bed, afraid of being buried alive and now suddenly in possession of a new terror: I was powerless against ghosts who could strangle me with a curtain sash or sweep their hands over my eyes and make me go blind).

Professor Stokes asks permission to perform an exorcism today, 6/27/18, the 52nd anniversary of the first episode of *Dark Shadows*, assuring Dr. Hoffman and Mrs. Stoddard that a supernatural presence haunts the Great House (which for some reason surprises Hoffman, who seems to have forgotten she once tried to cure a man cursed to vampirism by a witch), but before Stokes can begin to cast out Collinwood's evil spirits, he must first thwart a blurry, chroma-key ghost hand that just floated out of the secret panel inside the walls of the Great House drawing room, prompting Liz to observe, "This is a similar stage set as *All My Children*: you walk through the double doors in Adam Chandler's house, just like you do in Mrs. Stoddard's house, and there's a staircase to the immediate right in the foyer, then another set of double doors open up into the great room, where there are tunnels in the walls that go throughout the house" ("Filled with secret passageways and a revolving door of servants," writes Mark Brennan Rosenberg in the *Huffington Post*, "the Chandler Mansion runs rampant with murder, adultery and revenge plots," a dream-pop candy store of daytime soap transgression for Liz, who spent 20 years—over 5,000 episodes—watching *All My Children* without knowing the Chandler Mansion was a mirror image of the Great House at Collinwood, except for the vampires, werewolves, ghosts, and premature burials that haunted my childhood)—and just three weeks later, on vacation in southern Florida, we will encounter yet another architectural doppelgänger (I can't be surprised anymore by this book's relentless doubling) during a visit to Liz's birthplace, Gainesville, where the current owners, Crystal and Eric, will give us a tour of her childhood home, steering us from room to room, a box of tissues in hand for Liz, who will be bawling by the time she walks into their eight-year-old's bedroom—Liz's bedroom when she, too, was eight, the year her family moved to Chicago.

I can do anything I like with this pencil because I possess it, and it does
whatever I want it to—

> Tell me where
> he is, David—
> look at me,
> just look
> at me, David—

I'm going to exorcise the ghost from this house tonight, and if you cooperate I can
help you: I shall attend to the ritual itself outside the house, and I want you and one
other person to stay in the drawing room while I begin the incantation at some point
outside—

> Now he is only
> with you
> and possesses
> you when it
> suits his needs,
> but someday
> he'll want to
> take permanent
> possession
> of you and if
> he's allowed
> to do that,
> then David Collins
> will no longer exist—

Suppose it no longer responded to my demands: I could discard it and find a new

one, or I might become angry and decide to *snap* it in two so that it would never be

able to function again—

> Human beings
> are living things,
> David, and if they
> allow themselves
> to become possessed,
> they become just as
> helpless as this pencil—

Don't worry, David, this won't hurt a bit.

I still miss Sarasota, walking every night with Liz along Siesta Beach in a silk-blue, post-sunset haze, our toes sinking into sand so fine and cool it felt like powdered sugar, which might be why I'm distracted rather than charmed by the flimsy plotlines and precarious special effects of tonight's botched hauntings, starting with Professor Stokes's dowsing-rod exorcism, which accomplishes nothing but to make Little David shriek—and make me want to dip my toes in the cinematic gutter with Linda Blair—another failed intercession by the only occult detective in daytime soap opera history (just 45 episodes ago, he summoned psychic Janet Findley and she promptly fell down the stairs and died trying to rid the Great House of the same spirits that Stokes assumes he can vaporize with a silly forked twig and a few angry incantations)—not that the show's ghosts fare much better tonight, the camera dollying through the Great House's empty drawing room in the final scene, its gaze eventually coming to rest at the top of the staircase in the foyer, where Quentin leans forward, the mutton-chopped specter utterly self-satisfied that he's driven the entire Collins family out of the Great House: he chased away everyone he's trying to haunt, and now he's all alone, a ghost without a purpose, stuck in a loop of his own cartoonishly diabolical laughter in front of stained glass windows backlit by the strobe flashes of another dry *Dark Shadows* thunderstorm. "Collinwood belongs to the ghosts now," Barnabas announces on a jittery night when icy cerulean candles lean unsteadily from his seven-branched candelabra in the Old House (eight more flank his glass bookcase, and six light the reading nook next to his fireplace) and Chris Jennings explains that he saw "a long-sideburned man in a frock coat" stare at the Great House and then disappear into thin air (Barnabas: "He knows where the children are") and Little Orphan Amy enters the double doors of the deserted Great House and asks the ghost of Beth

Chavez to help her find the nineteenth-century telephone with severed wires that Maggie stashed in her room after she caught Amy and David using it to contact the spirit world (David: "Why is she taking so long? What if Quentin stopped her?") and Carolyn shrugs her brown minidress in front of Chris's crackling fireplace ("The mysterious Mr. Jennings," she says, "who announces he's leaving for no reason at all, then decides to stay for no reason, either," perfectly summing up the rickety logic of every *Dark Shadows* plotline since I began this impossible object of a poem) and in the last minute of tonight's episode—and last words of this book—the gauzy strings of "Quentin's Theme" drift through Little David's open bedroom window as the antique telephone simultaneously rings, a discordant combination of nineteenth-century Victrola tune and industrial phone-clang that wakes the psychic child from a restless sleep, the lime-green candlesticks on the double-branched candelabra next to his bed matching the color of his rumpled blanket ("How pretty the music sounds," Amy says of the soon-to-be-Grammy-nominated waltz that has become, for me, an irritating companion to Josette's music box, whose ice-cream truck melody first appeared 459 episodes ago and is scheduled to return 16 episodes from now, after the show makes a time-traveling narrative leap into the late nineteenth century).

Index: This Book's Relentless Doubling

Credits

(1968-69)

Barnabas Collins..Jonathan Frid
Elizabeth Stoddard Collins (Mrs. Stoddard)....................................Joan Bennett
Roger Collins...Louis Edmonds
Carolyn Collins Stoddard ....Nancy Barrett, Diana Walker
Ghost of Quentin Collins ....David Selby
David Collins ("Little David, the psychic child") ....David Henesy
Sarah Collins ("Ghost Girl")...Sharon Smyth
Cassandra (Blair) Collins..Lara Parker
Nicholas Blair..Humbert Allen Astredo
Victoria (Vicki) Winters...Alexandra Moltke, Betsy Durkin, Carolyn Groves
Maggie Evans..Kathryn Leigh Scott
Joe Haskell..Joel Crothers
Willie Loomis...John Karlen
Dr. Hoffman..Grayson Hall
Tony Peterson ("Lawyer Peterson")..Jerry Lacy
Professor Stokes..Thayer David
Jeff Clark..Roger Davis
Adam...Robert Rodan
Eve...Marie Wallace
Amy Jennings ("Little Orphan Amy")......................................Denise Nickerson
Chris Jennings...Don Briscoe
Tom Jennings ....Don Briscoe
Ghost of Beth Chavez ....Terry Crawford
Madame Janet Findley..Cavada Humphrey
Ezra Braithwaite ....Abe Vigoda
Mrs. Johnson ....Clarice Blackburn
Harry Johnson...Craig Slocum
Sheriff Patterson ....Vince O'Brien
Ned Stuart ....Roger Davis

(1795-96)

Barnabas Collins...Jonathan Frid
Jeremiah Collins ....Anthony George
Josette du Prés ....Kathryn Leigh Scott
Countess Natalie du Prés...Grayson Hall
Angelique Bouchard..Lara Parker
Victoria Winters ....Alexandra Moltke
Reverend Trask ....Jerry Lacy
Ben Stokes ....Thayer David
Peter Bradford ....Roger Davis
Navy Lieutenant Nathan Forbes ....Joel Crothers

Tony Trigilio is the author and editor of 12 books, including, most recently, *Inside the Walls of My Own House* (BlazeVOX [books]), the second volume of *The Complete* Dark Shadows *(of My Childhood)*. His books of poetry include *White Noise* (Apostrophe Books) and *Historic Diary* (BlazeVOX [books]), among others. His selected poems, *Fuera del Taller del Cosmos*, was published in Guatemala by Editorial Poe (translated by Bony Hernández). He is also the editor of *Elise Cowen: Poems and Fragments* (Ahsahta Press) and the author of the critical monograph *Allen Ginsberg's Buddhist Poetics* (Southern Illinois University Press). Trigilio coedits the journal *Court Green* and is an associate editor for *Tupelo Quarterly*. He lives in Chicago.

Made in the USA
Monee, IL
07 July 2026